The Complete Guide to Vegetable Growing

Peter Blackburne-Maze

D0531376

THE CROWOOD PRESS

First published in 1989 by
The Crowood Press
Ramsbury, Marlborough,
Wiltshire SN8 2HR

www.crowood.com

© Peter Blackburne-Maze 1989
Paperback edition 2010

ISBN 978 1 84797 174 6

Line drawings by Claire Upsdale Jones.
Colour photographs by the author.

Typeset by SR Nova Pvt Ltd., Bangalore, India
Printed and bound in Spain by Graphy Cems

Contents

well, but increasing. Nor is it just a phase; it's here to stay.

This inrush of foreign 'delicacies' has not, I'm happy to say, been at the expense of our traditional vegetables; it has been in addition to them. Carrots, parsnips, Brussels sprouts and other traditional British vegetables are as popular as ever, because a lot of foreign vegetables have one big problem: it's not always easy to grow them in the British climate. A lot can be done to shorten the odds, though, as we shall see.

Of course, our determination to succeed is increased by the difficulty of being able to find in the shops the vegetables we want, when we want them, and in good condition. Gone are the days when we were happy with limp lettuces and flaccid, yellowing cabbages because they were the only thing we could buy. Nowadays, the customer is beginning to tell shops what they can do with shoddy goods, edible or otherwise! Exotic produce is also more in demand and, if we can't buy them, we grow them. In spite of the rather illogical dislike that some people still have of the 'impersonal' supermarkets, they are usually second to none where the quality and choice of fresh food is concerned, and this most certainly includes vegetables. They demand the highest standard of their suppliers; and they get it.

And don't forget, no one is forcing you to buy from supermarkets. More and more farm shops and farmers' markets are springing up to meet the demand for 'natural'-tasting vegetables.

However, growing your own vegetables is often the only way of getting exactly what vegetables you want. To this can be added the freshness factor. How much nicer any vegetable tastes, especially salad, when it's crisp and fresh. If you'd like a lettuce for lunch, you go out and cut one and it's eaten and all gone within a few minutes. What could be nicer? Nor do you need a garden to achieve that; we'll be seeing how growing-bags can bring gardening to the gardenless gardener. Without wishing to put you off in any way, there's also the fitness and exercise aspect of gardening. If you didn't think there was too much exercise, half an hour digging clay or push-mowing a large lawn could change your mind! Finally, of course, there's all the pleasure and sense of achievement in producing your own vegetables.

That more or less ends the 'commercial' for growing your own vegetables; now we get down to the nitty-gritty, and the first thing to get into your head is that growing vegetables is easy. In fact, the hardest part is realising just how easy it is! That isn't to say that you can be slapdash about it and expect success whatever you do. Far from it; gardening is one thing where the results are directly proportional to the input. The more you put into it (provided that it's the right thing), the more you get out.

More and better gardening tools are also playing a part in making gardening easier. There's still plenty of rubbish about but I'll tell you how to spot that later on. We have far more greenhouses than ever before, and this enables us to raise many of our own plants and to grow unusual crops, or familiar crops at unfamiliar times of year. Along with this is the enormous improvement in seed quality and the range of varieties available; I sometimes think the choice is too wide and bordering on the bewildering. Still, better that way than having too little choice.

1 The Effect of the Site

Where you live and where the garden is may not at first appear to have much to do with gardening but it really is basic to the whole question and is entirely responsible for making it either pleasurable or a chore. To begin with, there are few of us who are able to choose where we garden or on what kind of soil. Both are usually dictated by where we work or have to live. This brings us to the not too surprising conclusion that there are good places and bad places in which to garden.

Most of us are lucky enough to live somewhere where gardening is perfectly feasible. The worst gardens are possibly those on very shallow soils; if there isn't a good depth of soil for the plants to grow in, the root systems will be poor and, consequently, the whole plant will suffer. Obviously one can improve this situation but it all takes a long time. Exposure to weather is another limiting factor although, as with terrible soil, something can be done to remedy it.

Many people would be inclined to think that gardening in a town is far from easy. In fact, towns, and especially cities, are usually a few degrees warmer than the open countryside. This can be a help. Also, established gardens contain far better soil than newer or more rural sites. This is simply because generations of gardeners have probably been improving the ground over many years. In essence, therefore, it's hard to think of a site that cannot be turned into a garden of some sort but, obviously, some locations are better than others.

The ideal, if such a thing is possible, would be in a position sheltered from prevailing winds on a gentle south facing slope. Much the same can be said about the ideal soil; however, the chances of finding one are remote. For the most part, though, there are very few gardens which cannot be improved to the point at which they will be productive. It's really a question of sorting out what kind of soil you have and knowing how to improve it, assuming that it needs it. One could fairly safely say that an 'ideal' soil is deep (I–2ft.), well drained and yet moisture retentive, supplied with plenty of organic matter, of good structure and with a medium texture. Don't worry about words like 'structure' and 'texture' at the moment, they'll be explained later, as will the whole subject of soil management (see Chapter 2).

The worst enemy of most vegetables is a waterlogged soil. The soil type itself isn't all that important, but it *must* be well drained. A soil which holds a lot of water invariably prevents sufficient air penetrating to the roots; and remember, roots need air to survive just as much as leaves do.

I mentioned that the ideal garden would probably be on a gentle south facing slope. This would allow cold air to escape downhill in the spring, thus reducing the damage done by spring frosts. It would also help drainage but, best of all, it would catch the rays of the sun at a more direct angle, and thus the soil would warm up quicker in the spring than will a flat site or one facing in another direction.

However, many gardeners are unfortunate in having a far from gentle slope on which to garden. Under these conditions, a few words of advice would not be out of place. The first is that, where it is feasible, the rows of vegetables should run *across* the slope. Sloping sites are often windy and across-the-slope rows are marginally better able to withstand the wind. Also, during heavy rain, rows running across will tend to trap the water so that it doesn't cascade downhill leaving those awful erosion gullies we often see on the television after tropical storms.

Because of the likelihood of wind, it is also a good idea to plant a hedge along the bottom boundary of the plot, and another across the centre if the area is large. Remember, though, to keep a few gaps in the hedge so that cold air can drain away in the spring, thus reducing the frost risk. Where possible, especially when the site is windy, try to avoid tall kinds and varieties of vegetables when there are shorter and sturdier ones available. The standard example here is broad beans; the 'Sutton', and now one or two others, are half the height of others and, with the spacing adjusted accordingly, you will get as heavy a crop from a given area as the old varieties. Runner beans can be a problem as well, but a way round their height is either to pinch the tops out to make them pinched beans or to grow a naturally non-climbing variety like 'Hammond's Dwarf Scarlet'.

Just because a garden is on a slope, it doesn't necessarily follow that it is a cold garden, but those in the midlands and north of Britain which face away from the south usually are. Here again, there are a few pointers that are well worth noting. The first is that a cold garden is also a late garden. For this reason it isn't a good idea to grow late maturing varieties of vegetables because

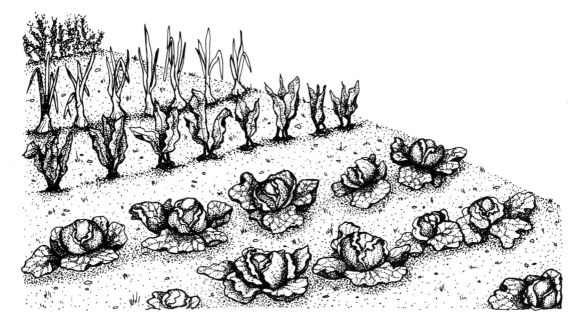

If convenient, always have rows running across a slope.

If your garden is in an exposed position, the first job is to provide protection from wind.

some may never make it; they'll run out of warmth too soon. Always, therefore, go for early varieties. An extension of this is that early varieties are normally the quickest to mature – they need the shortest growing season. Whilst this is useful in any garden, it is especially important in a cold one. Next, never put half-hardy plants out too soon in the spring in a cold garden or you run the risk of them being caught by a late frost.

It seems incredible, but gardens on opposite sides of the same hill can be one to two weeks different in maturity times. One thing that gardeners can do quite easily is to use cloches and polythene tunnels in the spring to bring forward certain crops in 'late' gardens. They can also be used to

advantage in the autumn when crops are nearing maturity but are slowing down. They can be covered to keep them going that vital bit longer.

Shady gardens can also present problems but their severity will usually depend on the source of the shade. If it is a building or a wall, there isn't much that one can do about it other than treat that particular area in the same way as one would a cold garden. The main snag is the lack of sun, which will usually make the shaded portion colder. However, if the shade is caused by overhanging trees, you could be in real trouble and it's worth thinking about the wisdom of growing vegetables in that particular place.

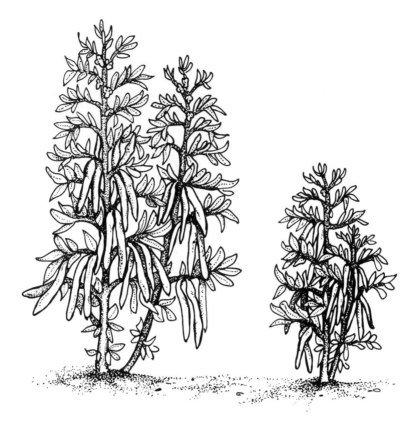

Shorter types or varieties of vegetables are preferable for
windy sites.

In this situation, the difficulty is fourfold. Firstly, there is the direct shading effect of the trees in reducing the amount of light that reaches the plants. This causes them to become leggy, drawn and weak.

Secondly, overhanging trees reduce the amount of water that reaches the ground by acting like an umbrella to light rain. This can be compensated by watering the patch, but it all takes time. There is also the problem of water 'drip' from the trees. This will mud-splash the plants and can, in time, puddle the soil surface and damage its structure.

The fourth problem is tree roots grow-ing into the vegetable patch and sapping the ground of water and what other little goodness reaches it.

Obviously a lot will depend on who owns the trees. If you do, you can do what you like with them, provided that they haven't got a preservation order on them. The first thing to do, assuming that you want to do something to reduce their effect, is to prune the top back to a harmless distance. If you can't do this properly yourself, get a good tree sur-geon to tackle the job. This is infinitely better than making a mess of it yourself, as bad pruning can often lead to the early death of the tree.

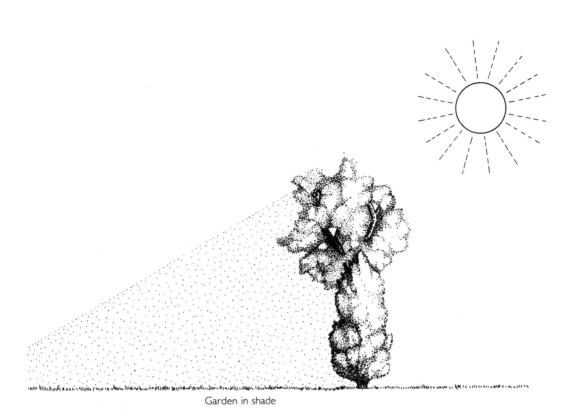

Garden in shade

Tall or dense trees or hedges may cause excessive shade and compete for water and nutrients.

The next thing to tackle is the roots and here you have to be a bit careful so that you don't sever any important support roots. If the trees are quite small, simply dig a trench about 2ft deep along the edge of the plot and cut out sections of any roots that you come across. Unless the tree naturally produces suckers, there's no need to bother about the roots in the vegetable plot; they'll die if they aren't still attached to the tree. In gardens where the trees belong to a neighbour, it's not going to be quite so easy and usually needs a summit conference to sort it out.

Regarding shade in general, the vegetables least tolerant of it are those whose fruits or seeds we eat, such as the pea and bean family. Because the crops rely upon the flowers being pollinated, they need the sun to bring out bees and other pollinating insects. Marrows also come into this category, and so do tomatoes.

No vegetable could be said to revel in the shade, but some will object to it less than others. On the whole, therefore, avoid growing them where there isn't plenty of sun because results will never be up to expectations. Far better to grow some of the many ornamental plants which thrive in shade and keep the vegetables in the sun.

Turning to exposed gardens, the problems with these are similar in that there are no vegetables which like being blown hither and thither by a strong wind. I've

2 ft (60cm)

Cut roots

Cutting roots of hedges. Throw the soil back in afterwards.

already mentioned the need to protect all gardens from strong wind. This is particularly important for vegetables on exposed sites as they're unlikely to fulfil their potential if they are constantly being battered by wind. The answer is to avoid growing tall kinds and varieties of vegetables or, if this is unavoidable, such as with Brussels sprouts and sprouting broccoli, to give the plants individual support. For runner beans, as I've already said, grow the non-climbing variety, 'Hammond's Dwarf Scarlet'.

When one considers the effect of the terrain on the climate of even a small area, one can often be surprised. For instance, many of you will know of districts where it can be raining on one side of quite a small hill and not on the other. I well remember living in one area where summer thunder storms used to follow a river valley right out to sea and then curl round and come back inland along another. Unfortunately, we lived in the centre, missed the storm, and still had the hoses going! There's nothing you can do about this sort of local curiosity but it's as well to be aware that it happens.

2 The Soil

We now come to the one thing above all others that will determine the success or failure of growing vegetables – the soil. There are very few things that all gardens could be said to have in common, but one is that they all contain soil of *some* sort. Soil is about as variable a material as it is possible to imagine.

It is at this point that people tend to divide themselves into those that take gardening seriously and those that do not. The 'not' group often refer to soil as 'dirt'. Let us have a closer look at soil and see why they are so wrong.

The first fact to grasp is that soil is a living thing, abounding with life in an almost unimaginable variety. Indeed, it is this life that makes a soil something that we can grow plants in as opposed to a desert, mud flats or a rocky ledge on a mountain. The life forms present in soil are a wonder in themselves and, in gardens, they range in size from something as large as a mole right down to microscopic bacteria and fungi. All have a part to play, and to ignore them is to start on a downward spiral that will bring us back to the desert or mud flat.

An unusually extreme example of this was nearly seen in East Anglia some years ago; and it still threatens those who don't heed the warning. The fields were getting larger to accommodate ever bigger machines and the hedges were disappearing. Dung and other bulky organic manures were no longer being used to maintain the soil's fertility; even the straw was being burnt after harvest. All that was being put on the land were inorganic fertilisers that fed the plants but not the soil. This led to what was known as the 'Fen blow' in which the topsoil was slowly being carried away from the fields by the wind. Followed to its ultimate conclusion, it could have resulted in the soil being virtually sterile and unfit for plant life. Don't for a moment imagine that I subscribe to the 'muck and magic' doctrine; I'm in favour of good growing conditions and, to attain these, you have to look after the soil, not just the plants.

Anyway, back to basics now; all soils exist in what are called three 'phases'. That is, everything that goes to make up a soil is either a solid, a liquid or a gas. By far the largest part of a soil is the mineral matter from which it is made and the nature of this is entirely dependant on what it has been derived from. We call that the 'parent material'; the clay, sand, chalk or other rock that underlies the soil.

The type and nature of the parent material also determines what a soil's texture and type is. Most gardeners are used to referring to soils as 'light' or 'heavy' and this is a reflection on what the soil is made from. For instance, a heavy soil is one with very small particles, such as clay or silt. A medium soil, the kind that we all wish we could garden on, is one with medium sized particles. You can find this anywhere, it often overlies rock. A light soil, on the other hand, is one that consists mainly of large mineral particles; typically sand.

The texture of a soil is more or less predetermined in that you have to put

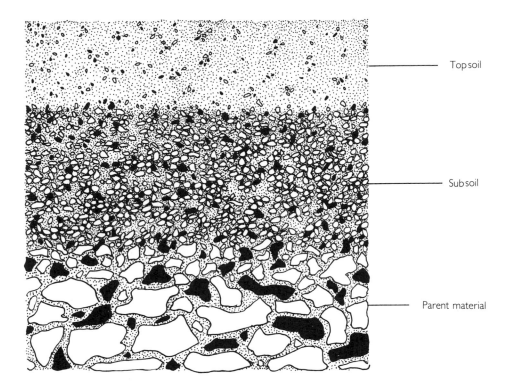

Top soil

Sub soil

Parent material

A soil profile.

up with what you are sitting on. We can do certain things to alter the texture on a small scale; for example we can import soil of the opposite sort to the one already present. It does, however, have a limited effect and should be considered only in an emergency. Something that we can do to improve the texture of a heavy soil, by employing the same principle, is to add horticultural sand or grit to it. This will open it up and make it better draining, but it really only forms part of the remedial action, as we shall see later.

Still with the 'solid' phase, we come to what is without doubt the most important constituent of any soil, the organic matter. Without organic matter, a soil is dead, because it is in this that all the microbes

and other minute forms of life exist. It is also the organic matter in a soil that helps to provide the plant foods that are so necessary for strong and healthy growth. Organic matter in the soil can, of course, be both living and dead. We have seen that the micro-organisms and other creatures, of various sizes, are one important group. The other is the vegetation; the fungi which live in the soil as well as the roots of plants.

Although the main functions of living soil organisms are to carry out chemical and physical changes in the soil, their death doesn't signal an end to their functions because it is from their dead remains that nature derives the nutrients for feeding the plants. It is, in fact, future generations of these selfsame micro and macro-organisms that decompose the remains, thereby releasing the nutrients.

Moving on to the liquid content of the soil; hardly surprisingly this is in the form of water. Clearly this is absolutely vital for the health and well-being of all the growing plants but it also has two other very important functions. One is that all the various soil organisms and micro-organisms are completely dependant on it for their existence. Many of them swim about in it and without it, at the worst, they would die. At the very best they cease to operate effectively in carrying out their vital work of breaking down the dead organic matter in the ground.

The other important job that water does in the soil is dissolve and transport the various plant nutrients. Indeed, without these being dissolved in water, they are completely unavailable to the plants. Plants can 'drink' the water but not absorb the solids. Water, therefore, is not only important in keeping all forms of life within the soil alive and active, it is also responsible for getting nutrients to the plant roots, and in a form that is usable by them.

In the final soil phase, gas, there are two that we are most concerned with: oxygen and carbon dioxide. Just as oxygen is the one gas that all living animals need, so it is also necessary to plants. It is not only needed by the above-ground parts of the plant; it is just as important to the roots. This is clearly shown when we consider a waterlogged soil. It is not the fact that it is full of water that does the damage, it is the lack of gaseous oxygen around the roots that causes problems. Water plants, like rushes and waterlilies, have adapted to this sort of existence but the vast majority of those that we grow in gardens have not.

Water is not the only factor to influence the amount of oxygen in the soil.

Compaction of the soil can have the same effect. Because there are not enough, or large enough, air spaces within the soil the life-giving oxygen is excluded. A compacted soil, of course, is also far harder for roots to penetrate.

Carbon dioxide is the gas which leaves absorb and turn into carbohydrates in the presence of light. It is also given off during the process of respiration (breathing), and the roots respire as well as the leaves. If there is a build-up of carbon dioxide in the soil because it cannot escape, due mainly to compaction, it follows that there is a corresponding shortage of oxygen.

Concerning air spaces in the soil in general, it must be remembered that it is via these pore spaces that water is able to escape downwards, or drain. If it cannot, the ground becomes waterlogged and we are back where we started.

I hope this look into what makes a soil 'tick' hasn't bored you because it is important to understand it if we, as gardeners, are to get the best from our gardens.

Having looked in simple terms at just what it is that soil is made of, the natural follow-up is to examine the different soils that we are likely to come across and how their performance is influenced by their ingredients.

We have seen that soil can be broadly divided into heavy (clay), medium (loam) and light (sand and peat). This is a simplification but it is perfectly adequate for our purposes. Let's start by looking at heavy soils, as it is these that many of us garden on and with which the most problems seem to be associated.

Heavy soils (clay and silt) are characterised by their small particle size (fine texture). This results in them frequently being poorly drained, and all that that implies by

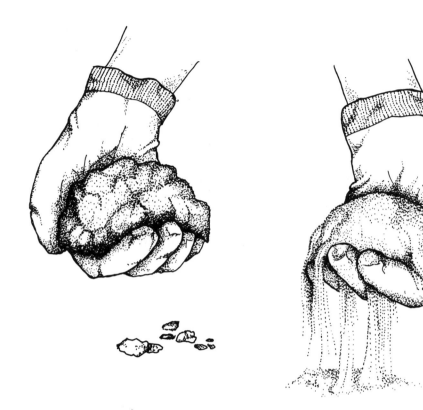

Heavy clay and light sand – the two extremes of soil. The perfect
loam lies somewhere in the middle.

way of the ground becoming waterlogged
more easily. Along with this is the likelihood that the soil will get compacted
easier and more often. Whilst this clearly
affects the drainage, an even worse result
is the difficulty with which roots can penetrate it. If a plant has to struggle to push
out sufficient roots to sustain it, growth is
unlikely to be good.

Heavy soils are slow to warm up in the
spring, mainly because of their normally high
water content. This is not always important
but it is worth remembering if early crops
are wanted. In a dry summer they have the
tiresome habit of becoming rock hard the
moment they dry out and, frequently, huge

cracks appear that you could disappear
down. Either that or, if they have been well
tilled, they simply turn into a mass of indestructible lumps.

From this, you could be forgiven for
imagining that heavy soils have a formi-
dable list of vices but few, if any, virtues. In
fact, this is far from the truth. Probably the
least obvious benefit of heavy land is that,
being firm and comparatively unyielding,
plants can get a very good foothold in it.
Once, that is, they get themselves established. Likewise, most plants will grow much
better in heavy soils because they have a
far greater reserve of plant nutrients and
moisture in them.

Taking these two things alone, once a plant, particularly a tree or shrub, establishes itself in clay, it is likely to grow far better than its companion growing in sandy soil. The water retention properties of heavy soils can also be to our advantage. We have seen that they hold a lot more water in the winter but this also means that they hold a good supply in the summer. They are, therefore, the last to dry out when there has been little or no rain.

At the opposite end of the soil scale are sandy soils. These are far less common than clay and, apart from little local pockets, they are found mainly in areas such as parts of Surrey, Bedfordshire, Cheshire, Lancashire and west Norfolk. In fact, they coincide with the market gardening regions of the country and it gives us an excellent indication as to their suitability for gardening; on the whole, they are first rate.

These soils are coarse and open textured and, as such, are very quick to dry out; rain that falls on them quickly drains away. Unfortunately, this also means that the water carries a lot of plant nutrients with it, so sandy soils are often starved, from the plant's point of view.

This quick-drying characteristic means that sandy soils have the advantage of warming up early in the year and are excellent for the production of early crops. They are also very easy to cultivate. Any plants that resent too much water are likely to thrive on sand, because of its drip-dry nature.

Another big virtue is the readiness with which roots are formed, and with which plants grow in it; hence its popularity with market gardeners. In a nutshell, once a plant is put into a sandy soil, it is up to the gardener how well it does; nature has done all it can. One thing to note is that, whereas clay soils can be either acidic or alkaline, sandy soils are always acidic.

Soils with a medium texture, not surprisingly, tend to have diluted versions of the advantages and disadvantages of clay and sand. They are as near perfect as one could wish for. They can be cultivated quite easily, plants grow well in them, they have a reasonable reserve of nutrients, they hold water well but have good drainage; in fact, they are everything that most gardeners would like.

Gardeners who are not blessed with this Utopian soil, and that covers nearly all of us, should never despair though; with time and effort, even the most unpromising soil can be turned into a first rate one that will do everything that is asked of it. The whole art of improving a soil to this extent is to do the right thing at the right time and always to be patient.

Although clay, sand and loam include the majority of soils in this country, there are several others that are found in certain areas. The most common of these is probably the thin soil that overlies chalk. This can be found in Wiltshire around the Salisbury Plain, through to the Chilterns and Hertfordshire and just into Cambridgeshire. There the band of chalk disappears underground, to reappear as red chalk in a small area around Hunstanton on The Wash in Norfolk.

Other well-known chalky areas are the North and South Downs of England. The soil above chalk is frequently thin and may, despite common sense telling you the opposite, be acidic. This acidity, though, is only in new gardens where the soil has not been disturbed. Under these conditions, there is usually a band of very organic and acidic soil at the surface. Once cultivations start and the soil is mixed up, the chalk imparts its alkalinity to this top soil. The texture of these chalky soils can vary greatly but is normally on the heavy side.

One of the advantages of this soil is that, due to the porous nature of chalk, it usually has good reserves of water. The chalk acts as a sponge and can hold a remarkable amount. At the same time, this porosity means that chalky soils are usually well drained. They may be wet clay on top but, underneath, there is very little chance of waterlogging.

Chalk is a fairly soft rock and, if solid chalk is near the surface, difficulties can be experienced in getting trees and shrubs established. The problem stems from the impenetrability of the chalk until fissures have been created in it for the roots to travel along. If your garden is overlying chalk and you want to plant trees and shrubs, it is necessary to break up the chalk to a depth of at least 60cm (2ft) with a pick or crowbar to give the roots a reasonable start in life. Once they have a bit of strength, they can usually manage for themselves. This problem is highlighted in beech woods on downland where nearly every gale has its victims. You can quite easily see the enormous platforms of roots with hardly any penetration into the chalk. Although we won't have quite such a severe problem with growing vegetables, the chalk must still be broken up to allow the roots to tap the reserves of moisture it holds.

Chemically close to chalk are the limestone soils of Derbyshire, the eastern half of Yorkshire and parts of Somerset. These have just the same characteristics as chalky soils except that they are usually much lighter in texture because the limestone breaks down into an almost sandy material.

Chalk and limestone soils are really quite common and newcomers certainly shouldn't be frightened of them. Much less common are peaty and fenland soils. These are normally found in flat, low lying districts such as south-east Yorkshire, the Somerset

levels and the Fens of Lincolnshire. However, they also occur in most mountainous areas, such as along the Pennines, in Derbyshire, Cumbria and many places in Scotland.

These highly organic soils are often very fertile and physically perfect for growing plants in, but they require careful handling if you are not used to them because they have very little reserve of nutrients and the high organic matter content is soon broken down once cultivations start. The peaty soils in the north are very acidic but the Somerset ones are less so because of the proximity of limestone (for instance around Cheddar) to the surface. They are the sort of soils that can often be improved by importing a heavier grade from outside the district.

The question of acidity and alkalinity has cropped up from time to time whilst looking at the different types of soil so it would be sensible to look at it in a bit more detail. Acidity, neutrality and alkalinity are expressed as the pH value of the soil. For gardening purposes, the scale runs from about pH5 to around pH8, with neutral being from pH6.5 to pH7. The lower the figure, the more acid the soil.

Most of the soils that we garden on are in the range pH5 to 8. Although the optimum pH for different plants varies, 6 to 6.5 is generally the area to aim at as this encompasses the greatest number of plants. It is slightly acid but not enough to cause any problems. All the normal sorts of vegetables that we're likely to grow in the gardens are quite happy with this.

The pH of a soil is really quite easy to alter; all that has to be done is to apply a material with the opposite reading. Therefore, if you garden on a strongly acid soil the answer is to apply chalk or lime, whereas gardening on chalk or limestone may necessitate heavy dressings of bulky organic matter, such as garden compost or farmyard manure or, in extreme cases, even powdered sulphur. These cases are extremely rare, though, and I can't recall seeing a garden which couldn't grow vegetables because it was too strongly acid or alkaline.

Where vegetables are concerned, very acid soils have more problems than chalky, alkaline ones. Just as a chalky soil will 'lock up' certain elements, so will an acidic soil, though not the same elements. Acidic soil conditions also reduce the population of, and therefore the beneficial effects of, many of the soil's micro-organisms. Because of this, the plants are not able to make full use of the naturally occurring plant nutrients as they are taking longer to break down into an available form.

The simplest way to reduce the acidity (or raise the pH) of a vegetable plot is to treat it with ground chalk, limestone or agricultural lime. In most cases chalk and limestone are better than agricultural lime because they are far kinder to any plants with which they come in contact. For this reason, agricultural lime is best applied only after winter digging, when it is going to be weathered and washed in during the winter and be gone well before anything is planted. Lime, does, however, have about double the corrective value of chalk or limestone.

Fortunately, there are fairly accurate guidelines as to how much chalk/limestone should be applied to a soil to have a given effect. As a rule, to raise the pH of a soil by 1.0, 500gm per sq.m (1lb per sq.yd) needs to be applied.

We have looked at what is meant by the texture of a soil and the effect that this will have on its nature and how well plants will grow in it. Now it is time to look at the meaning of another word – structure. This is often confused with texture and one is frequently used when the other is meant. Whereas the texture of a soil refers to the size of its individual soil particles and its true character, the structure is exactly what it implies; the way in which the soil particles are put together.

To illustrate this, imagine that the individual soil particles are represented by marbles. These are of different sizes but in heavy soils they would be predominantly small whilst in light soils they would be large. We now put the marbles into polythene bags and pack these into a huge crate. If the 'bags' are very large and the marbles are mainly small, as in the case of clay soils, there will be very little room for air in the bags or crate. There will also be hardly any spaces for water to drain through if it rains so it will tend to lie on the top layer of bags.

At the opposite end of the scale, we would find a sample of predominantly large marbles representing a sandy soil. These would be packed in small bags. When placed in the crate, there would be a large amount of air between the bags, as well as between the individual marbles. Air can flow through the crate quite easily, as can water, and in this soil structure roots can grow more or less unhindered. This is called a 'loose' structure and, as you can imagine, it has its problems just as much as a tight (clay) structure.

When we come to the medium textured soil, we find that not only are the marbles just about an equal mix of large, medium and small, but so also are the bags into which they are packed. This gives a soil that is truly between the two extremes with, one hopes, the virtues of both.

We have seen that the texture of a soil is very difficult to alter as it would mean adding marbles of different sizes and hoping that they would get into the bags and alter their size and shape. However, it *is* perfectly possible to improve the structure of the soil. Nature's way of doing it is to return dead vegetation to the ground and encourage it to be integrated not only into the polythene bags but also around and between them. This dead vegetation has the remarkable ability to bind together loose-structured sandy soil and break up clay and silt. In the former case it enables the soil to hold more water and plant foods; in the latter, it allows water to drain away easier and so improve a soil that hitherto lay wet. Thus, the structure of all soils is improved, whether they be heavy, medium or light. However, the dead vegetation, or organic matter, does not last for ever in a soil. The more there is, the greater the population of micro-organisms and, hence, the faster the organic matter is decomposed.

The end result of this process of decomposition is a substance that is known to, but not always understood by, all gardeners – humus. Humus isn't just another word for organic matter. It is a very mysterious substance that has a mainly chemical role in the soil rather than the largely physical effect of organic matter it originates from.

All soils contain both organic matter and humus and the level of both must be maintained if plants are to grow properly. From the gardener's point of view, there is little we can do to add pure humus to the soil, but a great deal can be done to increase the organic matter content, which will ultimately break down into humus. The effect that organic matter has on the soil, as has already been touched upon, is that it opens up heavy soils, binds together sandy soils and generally improves the structure and fertility of all soils.

We will be looking at the sources and effects of organic matter on the soil in more detail later. For the moment, therefore, we will leave it and turn to the different ways in which certain problem soils can be tamed and converted into something useful, though organic matter also plays a major role in this.

PROBLEM SOILS

Clay

The soils that most people have problems with are the heavy clays. These, as we have seen, have a tendency to go rock hard in the summer and become like putty in the winter. As an old farmer friend of mine used to say, 'All you do is break tools on it in the summer and change its shape in the winter'. That just about sums up clay. He also claimed that it only needed a black cloud to pass over it to make it unworkable!

The thing to remember about clay is that it holds a far greater amount of moisture and plant nutrient than you will find in a lighter soil. This makes it much better for gardening on, but you have to learn how to deal with it. The one thing you must never do is try to battle it out with clay; you don't stand a hope of winning and you'll have a miserable time gardening – people who like having their own way should steer clear of clay.

There are two very important features of clay that you must take advantage of whenever you can. The first is that the alternate action of freezing and thawing will break it down into a workable condition. The second is that wetting and drying will have just the same effect.

Most gardeners know that, by digging clay in the early winter, the weather reduces it to a fine tilth by the spring, admirably suitable for seed sowing. This is what has given rise to such twee sayings as

21

'The frost is God's plough'. The wetting and drying trick isn't nearly so well known but is really more important because we can use it throughout the growing season. This is especially handy after a crop has been cleared and the ground dug. If you try to beat clay into submission to form a seed-bed, you'll fail. Even a Rotavator will simply make the lumps smaller, it won't create a tilth. After digging, though, if the land is left until it is drying out following the first lot of rain, you'll find that, caught just right, it'll fall to pieces at a touch.

Another point to bear in mind is that, even making use of the wetting/drying trick, clay should never be dug deeply except in the autumn when it has plenty of time to weather. Fetching great lumps of raw clay to the surface in the summer is simply asking for trouble. Keep all cultivations as shallow as possible at this time.

That is the short-term way in which to treat clay and other heavy soils. The golden rule with them all is never to try to cultivate them unless they are in a fit and dry condition. If, when walked on, mud sticks to your shoes, don't touch clay. Leave it to dry out a bit more. All you will do when it's wet, as we have seen, is change its shape. The long-term answer to clay is bulky organic matter. One sometimes hears people who don't really know what they're talking about say that organic fertilisers, such as hoof and horn, will put clay right. This is absolute nonsense. A material of that sort is being applied at a few ounces per square yard. Bulky organic matter, such as garden compost, is the only answer and we're talking in terms of several pounds per square yard. The more the merrier. This will open up the clay physically by introducing new and softer material to it which will eventually break down into humus, the miracle chemical.

Humus atone isn't sufficient, however. We need the strawy and stalky material to open it up physically so that water drains away better and the clods are reduced in size. Added to this physical effect on the clay, some forms of bulky organic matter, when they have rotted down, will add to the ground quite useful amounts of plant foods.

On clay soils, any form of bulky organic matter (usually garden compost or farm-yard manure) should be dug into the vacant vegetable plots during the autumn. This will give the clay all winter to weather and will help to improve the drainage during what is usually the wettest part of the year. That is the normal way of adding organic matter to the ground but another system, though seldom used amongst vegetables, is as a mulch.

There are several things which will not improve clay at all. The first is the addition of gravel or sharp sand on anything but a very local scale. The amount needed to do any good to a reasonable depth is so enormous that the cost prohibits it. Just to give you an idea, to improve the top 6in (15cm) of soil, you would need to work in at least a 2in (5cm) layer of sharp sand, and preferably more. The best way to use proper garden sand (not building sand) is to mark out exactly where the rows of seeds are going to be sown and sprinkle the sand along this. It can then be raked into the top inch or so prior to making the drill and sowing the seed. This will greatly improve the condition of the soil in which the seeds have to germinate and none of the sand will be wasted.

The other 'don't' is in connection with peat and much the same rules apply as to sand. By far the best way of using peat (preferably sedge, used potting compost or old growing-bags) is to spread it along the sowing or planting rows and work it into the surface. Personally I'd rather use peat than sand. The next problem soil is completely the opposite to this.

Sand

The main trouble with a sandy soil is that it doesn't retain water or plant nutrients for more than a short time. This tends to make sandy soil starved and dry. It is, though, excellent for growing vegetables in, especially root and salad crops. Provided that they are given sufficient water and feed, they thrive on sand. The coarse texture of sand makes it easy for roots to penetrate and, thus, for transplants to establish quickly. It can be cultivated in any way you like under all conditions except when it's actually frozen solid!

In spite of these virtues, it is a difficult soil to get the best from, as a lot needs to be put into it, both materially and by way of work. The main aim of anyone gardening on sand must be to do everything possible to increase the water-holding capacity of the soil, and hence the nutrient level. Here, we come back to our old friend, bulky organic matter. As with clay, the best way of incorporating it into the soil is by digging it in but, and this is important, digging should be left until just before you want to use the land in the spring. The last thing we want to do is sharpen (increase) the drainage by breaking up the soil and adding drainage material in the autumn.

In fact, sandy soil should normally be left undug during the winter so that it can retain as much moisture as possible. Also, after digging, tread the land down firm again as soon as you can to reduce evaporation as far as possible. Much the same goes for any cultivations carried out on sand; it should be firmed back again soon afterwards.

Apart from the obvious need to water vegetables growing in sandy soil regularly, there is also the business of feeding them. In addition to the normal base dressing of fertiliser given before sowing or planting, a top dressing should be given about halfway through the plant's life, or when peas and beans start cropping. To reduce the inherent acidity of sandy soils and to improve the nutrient uptake in the plants, you will need to lime the ground periodically during the winter.

Chalk

The only other tricky soil present in large amounts in the UK is that overlying chalk. As was said earlier, this is often thin and starved and the main job a gardener has is to increase its useful depth to 12in (30cm). You should never try to do this all at once because, if the soil is overlying solid chalk rock, all you'll do is ruin what you have already got.

The way to tackle the job is by double digging the ground (see page 72) so that the topsoil and subsoil remain in separate layers. By incorporating garden compost or manure into the bottom layer, its fertility is built up over the years and it becomes useful to plants. When digging a chalky soil, always be careful not to fish up great lumps of raw chalk; too many of these will make it impossible to reduce the soil to a suitable tilth for gardening in.

There are, of course, occasions, usually when the soil is heavy clay, when an alternative to back-breaking labour is called for. At such a time, the 'deep bed' system of cultivation usually provides the answer. There's nothing mysterious about this and anyone can set it up. In its simplest form, it is just a series of beds with paths between them rather

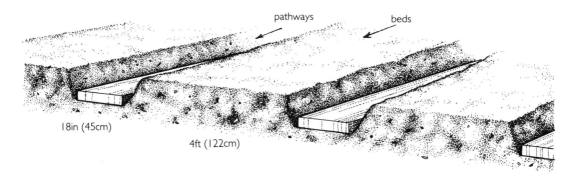

pathways   beds

18in (45cm)

4ft (122cm)

The deep bed system. Very useful on heavy ground and for making maximum use of the land.

than one large area of cultivated land. In fact, bed systems of one sort or another have been in use for hundreds of years on a more commercial scale. The whole point of these beds is that, once they are established, they are never walked on at all; the paths between them are used for everything. This means that the soil in the beds stays in an open and workable condition the whole time. Its structure is never under threat and can go on improving year by year. The only hard work is right at the start when the whole area to be taken up by the beds is double dug. This is necessary to establish a good foundation to the beds, especially as regards drainage.

During the digging, garden compost or manure is incorporated into both the top and bottom spit (layer) of soil. Inevitably this will cause the soil level to rise but, if done before Christmas, it will have settled back by the spring. Then, in about March, the area is marked off into beds 4ft (1.2m) wide, 18in (45cm) paths between each. These paths will be used for all walking, working and picking so that the beds are never trodden on.

Another innovation in the bed system is that, because they are only 4ft wide,

root crops such as carrots and turnips can be sown broadcast rather than in rows. This gives a far greater crop for a given area. If you don't want to give the whole bed up to one particular vegetable, you just put down as much as you want and keep the rest for something else, or for successional sowings.

Another trick is to have the rows running across the beds instead of along them; this is another way of getting heavier crops from a given area. Spacing can also be tighter. If the recommendation for leeks is, say, 6in (15cm) between plants and 12in (30cm) between rows, this can be brought to 8x9in (20x23cm) because you don't need the wider row spacing for walking in.

You'll notice, though, that the result of multiplying the two plant and row spacings in imperial measurements come to the same, i.e. 72sq in. This is because each plant still requires the same amount of space to develop fully; it's just that the 8x9 row spacing is far neater and more convenient for the bed system. Remember also that, where the plants in a row are staggered with those of the previous row (each plant is opposite a gap rather than another plant), the spacing between the rows can be the same as that between the plants within the row. This is particularly useful for cabbages and cauliflowers, but take care not to 'lose' one plant in alternate rows.

If the preparations were thorough and the ground was well enriched with bulky organic matter, the beds should last for 3–4 years without further deep digging. They should, however, be lightly forked over, incorporating garden compost, after each crop and given fertiliser in the usual way.

The system of double digging reduces drastically the amount of deep cultivations needed and makes the best use of the available space. It is not the same as the deep compost, no-digging bed system that is sometimes practised by, mainly, organic gardeners.

The really keen gardener who likes early crops can tilt the beds to the south by up to 10 degrees so that they catch the maximum amount of sun and warm up quickly. In areas of high rainfall, the tilting can also help drainage but a greater benefit in this respect is to have the beds raised a few inches above the paths. Remember to wear boots, though – the paths may be under water for much of the winter!

3 Planning

One of the first things that aspiring vegetable growers must get into their head is that planning is an essential part of the operation. This doesn't just include the cropping programme that it's necessary to draw up each year but it means, for a start, that you must sort out at a very early stage just what part of the garden the vegetable plot is going to occupy, and how much of it. Some people, indeed, won't want to bother with vegetables at all. In addition to all this, the spacing of the vegetables has to be worked out along with successional cropping so that everything doesn't reach maturity at once followed by a long gap.

So you see, it's one thing to own a garden and to grow plants in it but quite another to use it to the limit of its ability. Most gardens have the capacity to produce a lot more than they actually do. It's not normally the standard of gardening that is responsible for any shortfall in efficiency but, purely and simply, a lack of forethought, a lack of planning.

Just sowing vegetable seeds and planting the plants is not enough; there must be some overall plan. In fact there should be two plans. One is a proper scale drawing of the vegetable area so that the position of every row can be worked out annually and throughout the season, and plotted in relation to all the others. Only in this way will the ground be used to the full. The other plan is the timing; when such-and-such should be sown, maybe planted and, certainly, gathered.

I said 'annually' a moment ago; a good system is to run off several copies of the vegetable plan so that you can keep them from year to year and look back on your successes and failures.

If all this sounds like terribly hard work, don't worry; it's the counsel of perfection rather than what you *must* do. It has to be done, though, if you really want to make the most of everything. Then there's the timing plan, or cropping programme, so that we know just how long a given crop is going to be in the ground, and what it can be followed by. If these two plans are drawn up together, the best use is going to be made of the land.

There is no need to go into all the different possibilities here as regards planning because you will find all the information you need when deciding upon time and space (in the horticultural rather than philosophical sense) in the chapters dealing with them. This, after all, is the essence of planning; what goes where and when. It also has to be borne in mind that different people will want to grow different things, so drawing up a general plan is full of pitfalls for an author.

Something that we haven't touched on yet is the need, or otherwise, for a greenhouse. This has to be considered under the geography of the garden and, hence, the planning. You must, therefore, include the greenhouse when drawing up the plan of a vegetable plot. If you haven't got a greenhouse yet but are planning to buy one, don't forget that it's normally a question of where it will fit rather than where you want it.

As regards the position of the vegetables in the garden as a whole, clearly one should try not to have them in the most eye-catching place, but it's equally silly to have the plot at the back of beyond, if it can be avoided. The reason for this may not appear to be too obvious in the summer but, if you have to trudge through the snow to gather a few sprouts for Christmas dinner, it will quickly become apparent.

The other important thing is that the vegetables should never be relegated to the poorest patch of soil in the garden. After all, it's the only feature which is likely to show a profit so, logically, it deserves the best, though don't get carried away over this.

Besides the greenhouse, other features which are normally best placed in the vegetable section are the composting area and any tool sheds. The compost area because it is from the vegetables that most of the raw material will be coming, and the tool shed for the sake of appearances and also its proximity to the area in most need of its contents.

Even in the minute gardens that many people are forced to make do with today, never try to mix vegetables and ornamentals. The whole thing ends up looking a mess and is neither fish nor fowl. Added to that, vegetables in the flower beds are usually eaten and, when this happens, unsightly gaps are left. Keep the two sections apart, even if it means having just a few vegetables at one end of a flower border.

There are, though, exceptions to this, a good one being runner beans. These can look quite at home and very pretty amongst ornamentals if grown on a tripod of long canes, especially if both red and white flowering varieties are planted together.

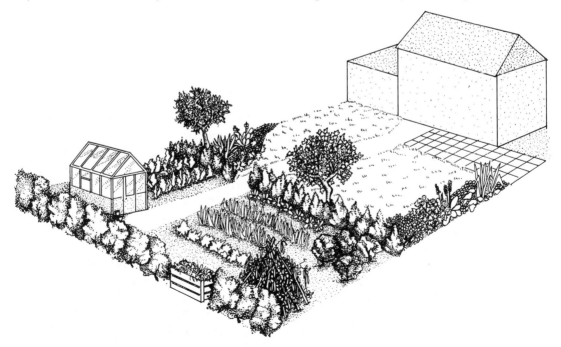

Normally, vegetables and ornamentals should be kept strictly apart.

If there is sufficient room, it's always best to have a physical barrier between the decorative and productive sections, and an evergreen hedge, such as a conifer, is one of the best. It provides a visual barrier all the year round as well as a windbreak for whenever the need arises. Do not, however, plant the ubiquitous Leylandii if the hedge is to be less than about 8ft (2.4m) high. It is very vigorous and will need clipping almost as often as the lawn needs mowing. Added to that, its roots suck the ground dry for yards around of any moisture and plant foods that they can find.

A line of cordon apples or pears are especially good; not only are they extremely productive, they also provide lovely blossom in the spring. However, there isn't much value in them as a windbreak in the early years. For immediate effect, panels of woven fencing (of the Larch-Lap type) are good because plants can be grown up them to give the impression of maturity. They make a good support for the cordons.

Once an area has been allocated to vegetables, the first consideration should be the direction in which the rows will run. North-to-south ensures that everything gets its fair share and maximum amount of light but it is more important that the length and direction of the rows are suitable rather than them having the best orientation. Dozens of short rows can be very tiresome to work amongst.

Perennial plants, like rhubarb and artichokes, should be grouped together as they will remain in the same place for a number of years. Many gardeners like to include strawberries amongst the vegetables; these should be treated as perennials as well.

Before sowing or planting anything, make sure that there is going to be room for it — hence the need for a plan drawn pretty well to scale on a piece of squared or graph paper. Where the vegetable garden is limited for space, concentrate on growing those vegetables which are unusual and difficult to buy or those which, for one reason or another, are expensive. For example, it is pointless to waste valuable land on something with as low a value as maincrop potatoes but it is perfectly in order to have a row or two of earlies to mature when shop prices are high.

Crops like peas and beans, especially runner beans, are always worth growing. Not only do they crop for weeks on end but, if there are more than you can cope with at any time, the surplus can be frozen. Remember also that some varieties of peas and broad beans are suitable for sowing in the autumn for maturing earlier in the following summer than spring-sown varieties.

INTERCROPPING

Intercropping, the practice of growing two or more different crops together is an important part of any cropping programme. The normal system is to have a longstanding vegetable, like Brussels sprouts, with a quick-maturing one, such as lettuces, between the rows of sprouts. The lettuces would normally be sown at the same time as the sprouts are planted out. In this way, the ground between the widely spaced sprout plants is not wasted and is producing a crop which, otherwise, you might not have had. The lettuces are out of the way long before the two crops interfere with each other.

A similar example is to plant alternate rows of late winter cabbages and seedling wallflowers. The cabbages go in at the recommended spacing with the wallflowers between the rows. By the time the two crops are touching (October/November), it's time for the wallflowers to be planted in their final positions.

There are many other examples of intercropping. Most involve growing quick crops between lengthy ones. A good one is to sow radishes, turnips or even lettuces next to and at the same time as a row of peas. They'll both grow together and, by the time the peas are ready for picking, the others will almost be finished, depending on which kind you have been growing. Sowing nursery rows of brassicas or wallflowers between rows of young plants and then lifting and transplanting the brassicas when they are large enough is another space saver.

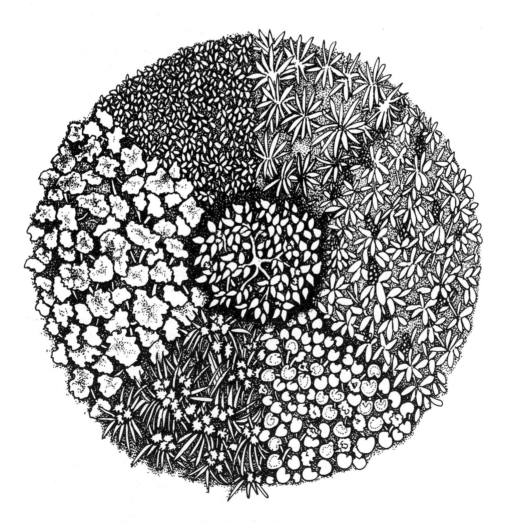

A very picturesque way of growing a good herb collection.

The whole art of intercropping is not to have tunnel vision and just use the technique simply to grow other vegetables. There isn't the slightest reason why flower plants shouldn't be raised in the vegetable garden; it is a very convenient place, in fact. Yet another thing which has to be considered is the use of growing-bags. I'll be covering the whole topic later on but they should certainly be taken into account at the planning stage because you can often make use of them to grow crops that you might otherwise have gone without, in places where you wouldn't normally dream of growing vegetables.

HERBS

Planning for herbs is an altogether easier job. Not only are there fewer to think about but they all tend to be there and in use at the same time so the sensible thing is to have them in the same place. As with vegetables, it is more convenient to have the shrubby ones and perennials together and the annuals, like parsley, in another group. The only thing that is important is that the herb area is as close as is reasonably possible to the kitchen door. There are few things worse than having to go to the other end of the garden in a thunder storm simply for a sprig of mint.

Herbs are becoming so much more popular today that they really do deserve to be grown properly and not just stuck in any old corner and left to get on with it. By this, I mean that they should be grown as plants in their own right and a complete feature can easily be made of them.

There are many good books on herb growing and all give excellent designs for herb gardens. One of my favourites is the cart-wheel design. In this, the bed is circular

and, preferably, surrounded by lawn, or better still by paving (for all-weather access). It is divided up into as many sectors as you want with a central circular area; this is kept fot taller plants, such as fennel, or woody herbs like sage. The lower-growing ones are planted in the separate sectors and all can be reached easily.

Herbs can also be grown in terracotta 'strawberry' barrels but be careful not to plant mint or tarragon in these as they'll quickly take over. Herbs are also first-rate in growing bags. As far as planning for herbs at this stage is concerned, simply decide on the design of bed or other growing method you want so that provision is made for it in the overall picture.

FRUIT

It isn't necessary to go too deeply into planning for fruit. To begin with, this is a vegetable book and, anyway, it is covered fully in the companion book *The Complete Guide to Fruit Growing* (Crowood 2010). However, an outline of the more important considerations must be given here.

Nearly all kinds of fruit can now be grown in dwarf or semi-dwarf form so it should never be excluded from a garden solely on the grounds of size and the room it would occupy. Besides that, fruit is very often grown in the vegetable section of a garden, so it has a definite bearing on vegetable growing. To give an idea of the life spans involved, bush and cane fruits can be expected to live productively for 12–15 years and fruit trees from 20–40.

Fruit should always be in a sheltered position which receives plenty of sun. If there is a choice, the north end of the garden is best as it can be in the sun and yet create no shade over other plants. Trees that are going to be trained to a wall or fence should face south or west to take full advantage of the warmer conditions. Later flowering varieties of apple and pear are quite happy against an east facing wall because the likelihood of sharp frosts is often over by the time they come into flower, depending on your district. The best-known fruit for growing on a north-facing wall is the Morello cherry, but cooking varieties of gooseberry and even apples are perfectly satisfactory.

If trees are to be grown as cordons in the open garden, the rows should preferably run north–south to give equal sun to both sides. If space permits, it is well worth setting aside a special area for fruit. This can combine free-standing as well as trained trees along with all the other types of fruit.

The management of fruit trees and bushes is much easier if they are all together and spraying can be done without risk to nearby vegetables that are, perhaps, ready for harvesting. Where it is possible to have a fruit area, there is no reason at all why, in its early years, it shouldn't also be used for growing vegetables between the trees and bushes.

In gardens where space is at a premium, a greater use should be made of intensive tree forms like cordons, espaliers, fans and spindlebush trees. In these smaller gardens, trees should be planted around the sides rather than in rows across the plot, where they might prevent the cultivation of the other plants close by. In very small gardens, and those where there is no soil at all but merely concrete or paving, fruit trees and bushes can always be grown but they have to be in large pots or some other decorative container.

CROP ROTATION

Possibly the final subject when discussing planning is the topic of crop rotation. It's never easy to know just where to include this as it also plays an important part in pest and disease control. However, careful planning is vital to the successful use of crop rotation.

Crop rotation is the practice of not growing similar types of vegetable in the same piece of ground for two or more consecutive years. That is to say, if Brussels sprouts are grown on a particular patch, then a crop other than a brassica is grown there for, preferably, three years.

In practice, vegetables (the only plants to which crop rotation really applies) can be neatly divided into three groups. By moving these around every year, a particular group will only be on the same plot one year in three.

Originally, there were two reasons for carrying out the system: firstly, to prevent the ground becoming starved of a particular plant food by having the same type of plant using the same nutrients year after year; and secondly, to avoid a build-up of any pests or diseases that were specific to one group of plants, for example, club root of brassicas and carrot fly.

The first reason, to prevent the depletion of plant foods, no longer applies. We have so many different mixtures of fertiliser that we can choose the one to apply according to the vegetables being grown. In this respect, it's well worth remembering that some crops need more of a particular element than others do. For instance, potatoes like plenty of potash, whereas lettuces need nitrogen. This is all dealt with later.

The second reason, to prevent the buildup of pests and diseases, is still applicable. However, pests are not so

Group 1 – Brassicas	Group 2 – Roots	Group 3 – Others
Brussels sprout	beetroot	peas
cabbage	carrot	beans
cauliflower	chicory	celery
kale	Jerusalem artichoke	onions
savoy	parsnip	leeks
sprouting broccoli	potato	lettuce
kohl rabi		peppers
radish		spinach
swede		sweet corn
turnip		tomatoes
		marrows

This is the ideal grouping for crop rotation but it is seldom possible. A plot is planted in year 1 with one group, year 2 with another, and year 3 with the third.

successfully affected as some writers would claim. They imply that, if, say, cabbages were attacked by the cabbage root fly in position A, moving them to position B the following year will reduce the problem. Clearly this is nonsense; pests are mobile and will search out a suitable host plant.

Diseases that live in the soil are a definite menace. These are usually fungus diseases like club root of brassicas, white rot of onions and parsnip canker. All are soil-borne fungus diseases and attack the underground (or near soil) parts of the host plant. Knowing that these diseases tend to stay in one place, it's common sense gardening to avoid growing susceptible crops on infected land for as long as possible.

Unfortunately, very few gardens are large enough to practise full and effective crop rotation; club root, for example, will lie dormant for seven years or more. However, anything that we can do to ring the changes, no matter how small the garden is, will be worthwhile, and this applies equally well to a small plot as it does to rolling acres.

The real point in question is whether crop rotation can be carried out effectively in a tiny garden. The answer to this is invariably 'No'. We can, though, take one or two elementary precautions as regards the worst soil-borne diseases, such as club root and white rot. Here, though, we are moving into the realms of pest and disease control so it's time to leave.

4 Tools

One of the most telling things about gardeners is what they keep in their tool shed and the condition that they're in (the tools, that is). Some are gleaming and have been lightly oiled so that they'll last for years and will always be ready and in good condition when they're wanted. Others will be caked with mud, rusty and in an awful state; worse than useless because they'll never do a job properly and will make hard work of everything. The owners are much the same!

As regards the different kinds of tool that you'll find hanging up, those gardeners who have been gardening for some years will already have their favourites and, apart from buying the occasional replacement or improvement, will be very conservative in the way they go about choosing and using them. What the new gardener has to learn first is that some tools are essential whereas others are expensive gimmicks that can well be done without. The hardest job is learning to distinguish between the two.

One thing that should always be borne in mind is that there is no such thing as a bargain where tools are concerned. Good tools cost a lot of money and any that appear to be cheap will be so for a very good reason. That reason becomes apparent soon after the tool has been put to use. The general rule is that you should always buy the most expensive tools you can afford; they will be the best. A good spade, for example, will last a lifetime; very probably two.

On the other hand, there seems to be an increasing number of tools which are stamped out of sheet steel and not properly forged, as they always used to be. The problem here is that, whilst they're certainly cheaper than the forged tools, and, to the untrained eye, look as good, they just aren't. Sheet steel is softer than forged steel and you'll very soon find this out when you're using, say, a Dutch hoe. If it's blunt and the land is heavy, it'll bend surprisingly soon.

Then there's the choice between ordinary and stainless steel. Stainless steel is certainly the best material for spades, forks and hoes but I'm not too happy with it for things like knives and secateurs; it never seems to hold a really sharp edge as well as ordinary steel. This may be imagination, though, because great advances have been made in hardening stainless steel.

Some tools, especially shears and other cutting instruments of that sort, can be made of ordinary steel coated with a special, hardened plastic that makes them virtually rustproof. They do, though, retain the keenness of edge that is not always attainable with stainless steel.

The most important thing to remember about tools of any sort is that, once they have been bought, they must always be kept clean and in good working order. Not only will rusty tools wear out sooner, but they will also be far less efficient at doing their job. Can you imagine a pair of rusty secateurs being any use at all? They won't cut the wood, they'll tear it and, in consequence, will often cause damage and leave a wound that won't heal over quickly. Result – often a fungal infection and die-back. And so it goes on.

A common fallacy is that stainless tools need not be cleaned – they should be kept just as clean as any other. Their main advantages are that they are easier to clean and the shinier surface tends, in the case of tools used for cultivating, to make them slip through the ground more easily.

Whenever any cultivating tool has been used, it must be cleaned straight away. One of the best implements for the initial cleaning is simply a piece of flat wood, something like a short ruler. This is used to clean off the worst of the dirt. It is then normally possible to wipe the blade quite clean with a rag. If the soil in your area is heavy, you may have to wash this remaining soil off. Avoid this if you can, though, because it then means that the tool has to be dried.

Finally, most tools will benefit from having the steel parts wiped down with an oily rag or paint brush. Don't overdo this, though, or you'll have drips of oil all over the place. Where possible, always hang up tools. It they're left standing on a brick or earthen floor, they'll probably go rusty at the point of contact.

If certain tools are not being used for some months, such as hoes throughout the winter, give them an occasional glance to make sure that they're still oily; it can wear off in time. Any tools that have been used in the rain must be thoroughly dried, and, if appropriate, oiled, before being put away. For what one might call 'general' gardening, the following are the basic tools that everyone will need.

SPADE

This is the main digging tool that is used for all primary and deep cultivations. It is the tool that is used both for breaking up new ground after the builders have left as well as the one that you will be using for the rest of your life in an established garden.

Use it for turning over the soil and for burying weeds and plant remains after a crop has been removed, and for incorporating garden compost or manure into the soil. It is not normally used amongst standing plants because of the damage it would inflict on their roots.

The spade is, if you like, the equivalent of a farmer's plough. It is suitable for use on all soil types although a digging fork is sometimes used in place of a spade on very heavy land, simply because it is easier to work with and does the job just as well.

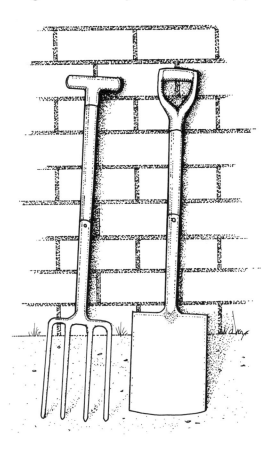

A spade and digging fork.

Spades can be made of ordinary or stainless steel. It is well worth buying a stainless one if you can afford it, but by no means essential, as it costs considerably more. Good spades will have a narrow step fitted to the top of the blade where the foot rests when digging. This is solely to prevent boots and shoes being ruined by continuous pressure on the otherwise sharp edge. It is the sort of refinement that turns a good spade into a first-rate one. However, if you use your heel to push the spade into the ground, and this often makes the work easier, the step is unnecessary.

It is also worthwhile looking for a spade in which the rivets which fix the handle to the business end run from front to back and not from side to side. Whenever a handle breaks, it is nearly always along the line of the top rivet of a 'side-to-side' model. A small point, but one worth remembering.

When being used for digging, a spade should always be held as upright as possible so that it works to the full depth of the blade.

FORK

This is normally used for shallower digging or, as already mentioned, for deep digging heavy clay. A common use is as a follow-up in the spring after a plot has lain dug and vacant over the winter. It is used to break up the clods as the first step toward creating a tilth suitable for sowing or planting.

A fork is also used for shallow digging amongst standing plants; it does far less damage to the root systems. It is the best tool for handling bulky organic matter.

Stainless and ordinary steel forks are available. Several different designs may be seen but most gardeners are quite happy with an ordinary digging fork. Incidentally, most tools, and certainly spades and forks, can be had in a variety of sizes to suit all uses and physiques.

RAKE

The rake is used almost exclusively for levelling ground and breaking the soil down into a fine tilth suitable for sowing in. The latter is usually done after the initial forking to break up the clods. A rake is also useful for incorporating fertilisers into the top two inches or so of the soil.

The extra cost of a stainless steel rake would be hard to justify. Lawn rakes with spring tines are a completely different tool and are not intended for working the soil, rather for raking out moss and other debris from the surface of lawns.

HOES

Dutch Hoe

The Dutch (push) hoe is the standard weeding tool and has been used by gardeners for generations. However, it has another important use; that of moving a shallow amount of soil either to prevent or to destroy a surface crust. The gardener moves backwards when using the tool and thus hoes out his footmarks as well.

This is another instance where stainless steel can have advantages over ordinary steel in that the hoe slips through the soil more easily.

The object of a Dutch hoe's action is to sever the top growth of a weed from the root system just below the surface; it should not be used to push or dig the weed out complete with its roots. If the soil is damp,

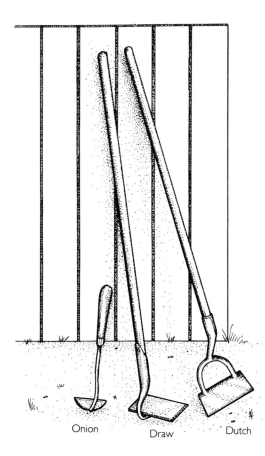

Onion, draw and Dutch hoe.

it will simply form new roots and carry on growing. For this reason, the cutting edge of the blade must always be kept sharp.

Hoeing during wet weather, or when the soil is wet, is normally a complete waste of time and can, in fact, cause harm by damaging the soil structure.

Draw Hoe

The draw (swan-neck) hoe is also useful for weeding but is used as well for drawing up the soil over potatoes, for drawing out seed drills, for working the soil shallowly and for thinning out rows of seedlings.

Unlike the Dutch hoe, you move forwards when using a draw hoe so it is normal to work to one side of it so that hoed ground isn't immediately walked upon. When hoeing between rows of plants, walk in the row to be hoed next so that you keep off the hoed land.

As with the Dutch hoe, always keep the blade sharp and use it as flat as you can so that it travels just below the surface and doesn't dig in like a plough.

DIBBER

An essential tool for planting out brassica seedlings. A dibber is used to make the hole in the ground into which the roots are put and for firming the soil back around the roots. The result is much firmer planting than could ever be achieved with a trowel or fork.

When planting brassica plants, a reliable test of their firmness after planting is to tweak a leaf. If the plant comes out of the ground, you aren't planting firmly enough. You are if the leaf breaks off.

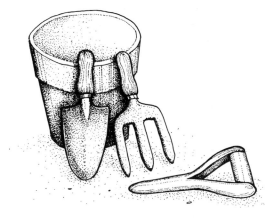

Trowel, hand fork and dibber.

You may sometimes see small wooden or plastic dibbers similar in size to a pencil. These are for use when pricking out pot-raised seedlings and are not the type we are concerned with here. The sort I am referring to is a much larger tool with a handle to push against.

You can make your own quite easily from the broken handle of a spade or fork. Make it about 15in long, sharpen the end and, if possible, sheathe the point with metal; this makes it far easier to push into the ground.

A dibber is another tool that should never be allowed to become rusty as rust will greatly impair it's efficiency.

GARDEN LINE

No good gardener will ever try to draw out a straight seed drill or put in a straight row of plants without a line, no matter how short a distance is involved or how experienced he is. The more experienced you are, the better you know that you need a line.

Plastic lines are normal now and are virtually indestructible; unless you happen to chop them with a spade too often. Orange plastic is a good colour because it shows up well. Make sure that both ends of the line are firmly anchored and that it is taut, absolutely straight, and is not resting on a clod of earth that kinks it.

When making a seed drill with a draw hoe, work backwards and keep one foot on the line to prevent it being moved off centre.

TROWEL AND HAND FORK

These are very useful for digging up or planting young plants and seedlings and for working to a shallow depth amongst standing plants in a confined space.

Don't overtax their strength by expecting them to do the same jobs as a spade or digging fork; this simply leads to breakages and usually a loss of temper.

MEASURING ROD OR STEEL RULE

A measuring rod marked off every 6in is extremely useful when planting out or thinning seedlings. You can easily make your own out of any straight piece of timber 4–5ft long by 1in square.

In fact, this kind of rod is of more use than a tape when thinning or planting in rows, but a tape is also useful to have for accurate measuring.

EXTRA TOOLS

I have mentioned the basic tools that you will need when growing vegetables, but there are a few more which will be found useful as you become more experienced and better able to judge what is needed.

Knife

This is a useful tool that can perform a hundred jobs about the garden. However, a blunt knife is an abomination. Not only does it not perform the task for which it is intended, but it is far more likely to cut you than is a sharp one. Make sure you get a strong knife with a good blade; toy knives aren't intended for gardening.

Hand Cultivator

These go under various proprietary and brand names but all do the same job, with greater or lesser efficiency. Their sole task is to break down dug soil into a suitable tilth for sowing or planting in, and nothing more. I mention this because, more than any other tool, 'improvements' have appeared with such monotonous regularity as to be boring. These are usually over-priced, too clever by half and certainly do no better job than the simplest design, if as good a job.

The most effective hand cultivator consists of four or five tines which are bent down and round through 180 degrees into something like a hook. You can make your own from an old digging fork on a hoe handle or you can buy rather more sophisticated ones with removable tines. Anything more complicated than that is completely unnecessary and likely to be too expensive for what it does.

You normally work backwards with a hand cultivator using a backwards and forwards motion until the soil has been reduced to the required tilth. It's a very useful tool for incorporating a base dressing of fertilizer into the surface soil before sowing or planting whilst, at the same time, forming a suitable tilth.

'Swoe'

This is a proprietary and patented type of hoe that combines the virtues of both the draw and the Dutch hoes. It has a stainless steel blade which is attached at one point only to the traditional hoe handle. This makes it similar to the draw hoe. However, the blade is held flat on the soil surface and is pushed backwards and forwards like a Dutch hoe.

Another innovation is that the opposite edge of the blade to the handle is flat and sharpened so that it can also be used with a sideways motion.

The Swoe is a useful tool that is the result of a lot of thought. Not at all gimmicky.

The patented 'Swoe' combines the benefits of both the Dutch and draw types of hoe.

You'll come across other tools from time to time as you walk round garden centres but you'll find that they probably all do roughly the same jobs as those you've already got so be thoughtful in what you buy and make sure that it really is what you want. There's little worse than spending hard-earned money on something which turns out to be no better than something you've already got which does the same job and which had been left in the tool shed by the people who sold you the house!

MECHANICAL TOOLS

Whenever the subject of garden tools is considered, it isn't usually very long before the question of what might be called 'mechanical aids' crops up. Just as there are gardeners who firmly believe that chemicals are a way of gardening, rather than an aid, there are also those who feel the same way about engines; whether they are driven by petrol or electricity. They cannot live without them – noise, smell and all.

A moment's thought will bring to mind a whole array of what are euphemistically called 'power assisted' gadgets. There are grass cutters for every quality of sward imaginable. You can cut hedges, you can chop up raw materials for composting (more about this later, see page 62), and, as for cultivating the ground, well, there are more machines than most of us would know what to do with.

How many of these machines, though, are really necessary and how many are just an expensive and often rather useless luxury that is played with a few times and then put in the corner of a shed to be forgotten until the next jumble sale? The answer probably depends on your circumstances, the depth of your pocket and your thoughts about the compatibility of machinery and gardening in general.

What all this boils down to is that people who buy machines tend to fall into one or more of three groups: those who want to flash it about and impress others; those who think, or who have been convinced, that a machine makes life easier or that a particular one is something that they cannot do without; and those gardeners who genuinely benefit from them.

Clearly it is the last group with which we are concerned here but, before buying a machine, it is a useful exercise to look in the mirror and truthfully decide which group you really belong to. It may not make any difference to the final decision but a little bit of self-examination is always revealing.

There may, of course, be a number of reasons for needing a machine but there are two that dominate. One is that there is simply too much work for one pair of hands to do without mechanical help, and the other is that, for some perfectly good reason, you do not have the physical ability to do the job in question. The normal reason is the disappearance of youth. These are the only two really valid reasons that justify buying a particular piece of machinery. Many would add to the above the fact that a machine does a job easier and quicker. I have my own thoughts on that.

The Rotavator

The machine that we would be primarily concerned with when growing vegetables is the Rotavator. It is safe to say that most models will do the job for which they are intended. Obviously there are exceptions but they are rare these days, as word soon gets round and they die a natural death. Machines that have been designed by engineers with little reference to gardeners are usually pretty easy to spot.

So really how valuable is a powered Rotavator? The not very helpful answer to this is that they can be both a blessing and a curse. Let's take their virtues first. The main one is that they make an excellent job of breaking down roughly dug ground, and in a lot less time than it takes by hand. This is not particularly important in a small garden but it can be a boon in a large one in the spring when everything seems to need doing at once and there is a big black cloud hovering overhead.

There is also no finer way of clearing the ground after one crop in preparation for setting the next. Everything is chopped up nice and small so that it can easily be dug in or just left as it is with the next crop being sown or planted without further cultivations. It is also particularly good at incorporating manure and garden compost evenly into the soil.

Even if it is sometimes rather like taking a sledge-hammer to crack a nut, a Rotavator can be an excellent tool for weeding between rows of vegetables or fruit. It should, however, only be used to a shallow depth for this purpose and only when the soil is dry. Also, just because a machine is doing all the work, this job must not be left until the weeds are a foot high and seeding.

Top of the list of misuses must surely come digging. There is not a single garden Rotavator that can fully take the place of a spade, and never let anyone try to convince you otherwise. For a start, very few will go deep enough, especialy on heavy land. All you can expect from the best of them is 6–9in (15–23cm) whereas we are talking in terms of 12in (30cm) to do any real good.

If used in place of a spade, many will break up the ground much too fine and create a puffy tilth. This is not what is wanted and, if ground in this state has to stand the winter, it will be mud in no time.

Another misconception about Rotavators, is that because all plant debris is smashed to pieces, this will kill it. In many cases it does, but not things like bindweed, ground elder and creeping thistle roots. If these are present in the ground a Rotavator is the finest way of spreading them about.

Lastly, and probably most serious of all, the continual use of a Rotavator can create a solid pan a few inches below the surface. This is caused by the blades smearing the soil at the same depth every time the machine is used.

Make no mistake, though, the Rotavator's faults are not usually created by the machine itself but by gardeners using them either to do jobs for which they were not intended or simply misusing them. One of the worst things you can try to do with a Rotavator is use it to beat the soil in poor condition into a good tilth. This brings us back to that business of battling with the soil. A machine may have the power to chew up the ground when it cannot be done by hand, but all it will do to a soil in this condition is destroy the structure.

To summarise, therefore, a Rotavator used sensibly at the right time and to do the correct job is a terrific help and can save a lot of work. In the *wrong* hands it can ruin the soil structure in no time at all and make gardening an unbelievable burden. Nor does it pay to buy the cheapest you can find. As with other tools, you get what you pay for. Always buy a robust make that is not going to fall to pieces once it is faced with hard work. If you're in doubt, it's always best to buy a model recommended to you by a knowledgeable friend.

5   Feeding Plants

The feeding of plants has always been a subject that every gardener knows about and appreciates but which very few actually carry out, and certainly not to the extent that they should. It's a bit like children cleaning their teeth; they all know it must be done and what happens if they don't, but most still think it's all too much bother and not worth the trouble; tomorrow's another day.

Can you wonder that many of the plants in our gardens aren't what they should be? This is particularly the case with vegetables because, in this part of the garden above all others, we want good results that are going to please us and save us money.

There is a slight divergence of opinions when it comes to feeding plants, especially vegetables, because this is the point at which the 'no chemical' gardener would begin to break away from what might be called mainstream or orthodox gardening. Anyone who does not intend to use chemicals will almost certainly frown on the use of what are referred to as artificial fertilisers.

'Artificials' are man-made plant foods, as opposed to those which occur naturally, but there is no clear dividing line between the two and it is left largely to one's conscience and preference as to which ones are considered ethical and which are not.

For example there can be very few fertilisers more natural in origin than hoof and horn, but where does basic slag fit into the picture? Slag is a by-product of the steel industry and used to be widely used as a phosphatic fertiliser. The phosphorus comes from the iron ore during the smelting process. It certainly is not an organic material and it isn't naturally occurring, but it seems to be acceptable in a way that, say, superphosphate isn't. We live in a strange world full of strange thoughts and ideas!

There are two equally important sides to the subject of feeding plants; organic matter and plant nutrients. They are completely separate but operate together and woe betide any gardener who thinks he can get away with ignoring either; both are essential for strong and healthy plant growth.

ORGANIC MATTER

As possibly the more important of the two is organic matter, we'll look at that first. We've already had a look at the part it actually plays but that was solely in relation to its effect on the soil rather than its origin and sources. Because organic matter is at the very heart of gardening, we'd do well to be aware of the different sorts that we are likely to find available and use. Broadly speaking, they fall into two groups; those that are bulky and which are used mainly for improving the structure of the soil, and those which are applied in small quantities as a source of plant foods. The latter we will be covering when we discuss feeding plants.

Farmyard Manure

In years gone by, the most common form of bulky organic matter was farmyard manure (FYM). Most of the gardening went on in the country where the supply was virtually limitless – what would be described nowadays as a 'renewable asset'. There's still no shortage of FYM but the number of gardens has increased so dramatically that there just isn't enough to go round. Added to that, there are now many more town gardens than there used to be so the problem of transport crops up.

FYM is still thought by many to be the elixir of plant life but science has taught us that this is far from the case and that there are perfectly good altenatives. The quality of FYM can vary greatly and this is due to a number of things. The proportion of straw or other litter will have an effect, as will the type of animal that produced the dung. The degree of decomposition will also influence its value.

By and large, though, an average sample of FYM (if there is such a thing) will contain approximately 76 per cent water, 0.64 per cent nitrogen, 0.23 per cent phosphates and 0.6 per cent potash. This may not sound very much as against the 21 per cent nitrogen contained in sulphate of ammonia, and indeed it is not, but it does represent a useful amount, and anyway FYM should be thought of more as a bulky supplier of organic matter rather than a nutrient source. It isn't the nutrient value of bulky organic manures but their physical effect on the soil that is important.

One thing that can be said for most bulky forms of organic matter is that they contain the trace elements.

Straw

Whilst FYM or stable manure is not always easy to come by, something that most of us *can* find is straw. The benefit of this is not just that there's a lot of it about but that it is also far easier to take home and a much less anti-social material.

Straw by itself is of little value to gardeners, but once composted it provides a good alternative to FYM. Nutritionally it compares quite favourably with it as well, having some 0.5 per cent nitrogen, 0.2 per cent phosphates and 1 per cent potash.

Sewage

Sewage sludge used to be a common material for spreading on the garden but we tend to take rather a dim view of it now – and yet we are quite happy to use animal manures. Raw, but dried, sewage sludge on its own is of low value as a soil improver, but when mixed and composted with straw it provides a valuable manure. A typical sample would contain as much as 60 per cent more nitrogen than FYM, about the same amount of phosphates, but rather less potash. It can be regarded mainly as a source of nitrogen and organic matter.

However, the supply and use of sewage sludge is now so tied up with rules and regulations that not only could it be difficult to find, but it may also be illegal to use it. In any event, there are plenty of alternatives, both as effective and easier to find, that don't carry the same problems.

Domestic Rubbish

Many local authorities are now collecting and composting garden and other suitable waste materials to form a very useful source of bulky organic matter for digging into the garden. It is, if you like, garden compost produced on a massive scale and, in many cases, better than you can produce at home. A word with your local council should quickly put you in touch with a nearby source.

Wool Shoddy

A typical analysis of this material would be something like 0.8 per cent nitrogen, 0.54 per cent phosphates and 0.43 per cent potash plus, of course, trace elements. Wool shoddy, the waste from the Yorkshire woollen mills, used to be a splendid form of bulky organic matter. It was a popular material in the hop gardens of Kent, where I grew up. Unfortunately, man-made fibres have reduced the amount of pure wool shoddy considerably, but it can still be had. The mixed grade of shoddy now being produced is by no means useless, however. The nitrogen content is reduced, but its physical effect on the soil is just as good, if not better, as the man-made fibres take much longer to rot than the wool.

The highest grade of pure wool shoddy would have a nitrogen content of 12–15 per cent. Lower grades would be 5–10 per cent and contain 75–80 per cent organic matter.

Peat

Like sewage sludge and wool shoddy, peat is becoming something of a 'product of a bygone age'. I have my own feelings about the arguments raging over its use in the garden, but this is not the place to air them. All I would say is that the Norfolk Broads are worked-out peat fields and you'll have a job to find a more beautiful or ecologically sound area. Nobody moans about that.

When one thinks of peat, it is normally as a constituent of seed and potting composts and as a material to use for improving the soil when planting trees and shrubs. It is not in the same class as FYM, straw or garden compost.

The trouble with peat is that the particles are very small so the physical effect on the soil is less than that of coarser materials. The nitrogen content varies from 1.5 to 2 per cent, phosphate about 0.03 per cent and potash 0.1 per cent, so you can see that its nutritional value is almost nothing. Peat's real worth lies in its acidifying action when applied to alkaline soils, and its help in the creation of a fine tilth.

The pH of peat may vary from 3.0 to 6.0, depending on its type (moss peat is the most acidic, sedge the least). The most valuable would be in the range pH4–5.

Pine Bark

A material that is increasing in popularity is pulverised pine bark. It has much the same uses as peat but is far longer lasting in the soil due to its hardness. This hardness also means that its physical effect on the soil structure is much greater. Not only does it provide organic matter but its physical condition is, in some respects, akin to gravel. When used as a mulch, there is little risk of it blowing about.

The plant food value is virtually nil but, with a natural pH of 4–5, it is another valuable, and longer lasting, acidifying agent. Beware of some brands if you are looking for the completely natural product as they may have additives to increase the nutrient value (and price) and reduce the acidity.

Mushroom Compost

Spent mushroom compost is readily available in some areas and it makes a useful soil improver. It consists mainly of straw composted with horse manure and with ground chalk added to raise the pH (and so reduce the acidity). Once again, the plant food value is low but it is valuable for its soil improving qualities.

One thing to remember about spent mushroom compost is that the chalk content usually makes it unsuitable for use amongst ericaceous plants. This will not matter when used with vegetables.

Woody Materials

Sawdust, wood shavings and chippings are all quite easily found in some areas as waste products from timber and furniture works. The worst thing about any woody materials is that they will rob the ground of nitrogen if applied 'raw' and uncomposted. This means that they should either be composted with other waste vegetation and an activator before use, or they should be applied in conjunction with a fertiliser containing nitrogen. This is because, during decomposition by microorganisms, a lot of nitrogen is used up.

Leaf-Mould

One of the most valuable sources of bulky organic matter is leaf-mould. In rural areas this is often quite easy to find but, before collecting it yourself out of woods, do make sure that you are allowed to.

In most woods, the best leaf-mould will be found a few inches below the surface as it will have lain there for several years and be well rotted. Freshly fallen leaves are perfectly all right but they should be composted for upwards of a year before they are fit for use.

Raw leaves will not only need nitrogen to rot down, like sawdust, but they will also blow about all over the garden if used as a mulch. Once again, the nutrient content is low but their value to the soil is high.

Seaweed

Near the coast, there has always been a strong leaning towards seaweed and it certainly does do a lot to improve the soil. Fresh seaweed has a similar nitrogen content to FYM but much less phosphate and about twice as much potash. It has the same organic matter value but rots down a lot quicker because of its physical nature and nitrogen content. In fact, it is excellent for adding to straw to rot it down quicker.

Seaweed has a useful amount of trace elements, principally iron, manganese and zinc. However the real benefit of seaweed lies in its alginate content. These extraordinary chemicals even have a number of uses in industry, but their particular interest to gardeners lies in their ability to improve the soil structure by opening up clay soils and binding together sandy ones. What seaweed therefore lacks in fibre, it more than makes up for in alginates.

Garden Compost

The last source of bulky organic matter that I will mention is the cheapest and most readily available of all. If you have a garden, then you are growing the raw material and it is sitting there in front of you – garden compost. We shall see later how easy it is to make and how to go about it, but here we are concerned with its value as a soil improver and supplier of plant foods.

Contrary to what most people believe, garden compost normally has a higher, plant food value than FYM: 2–2.5 per cent nitrogen, 0.5–1 per cent phosphates and

0.5–2 per cent potash. This makes it a very valuable manure. Obviously the figures are extremely variable because they depend entirely on what the compost is made of, but these are the average readings.

Because the amount of fibrous material also varies greatly, the soil-improving value of garden compost is rather unpredictable but the average sized garden will have enough raw material to make composting worthwhile – and it costs virtually nothing.

That more or less covers the various sources of bulky organic matter. As we have seen, all the various forms do contain plant nutrients to a greater or lesser extent but none have enough to dispense with the need to add specific nutrients to the soil. The problem is that nature is a complete cycle with everything returning to the ground and being used by the next generation of plants. These, in turn, die and are returned to the soil to be broken down; and so on.

In gardens this doesn't happen. The moment we start to grow crops for eating, we inevitably break the cycle because we are not putting back what we are taking out. We therefore have to return it in some other form and, in the case of plant nutrients, the conventional and convenient way is with fertilisers.

It is quite impracticable (and impossible) for most of us to rely solely on compost or FYM. For the 'organically' minded, the choice of naturally occurring materials that contain sufficient plant foods to be called fertilisers is, fortunately, large so there is plenty to choose from.

However, that's rather jumping the gun, because we should firstly look a bit closer at just what plant nutrients are. There are twelve elements that are absolutely essential to a plant if it is to be strong and

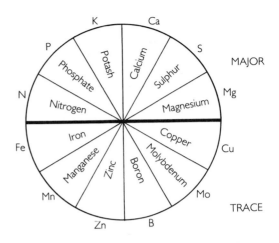

The twelve elements essential for healthy plant growth.

healthy. These can be divided neatly into six major elements and six trace elements. The major elements are nitrogen (N), phosphorus (P), potassium/potash (K), magnesium (Mg), calcium (Ca) and sulphur (S). The trace elements are manganese (Mn), iron (Fe), copper (Cu), zinc (Zn), boron (B) and molybdenum (Mo). The word 'minor' is sometimes used instead of trace to describe the latter but this can be misleading as it could imply that they are of minor importance. Nothing could be further from the truth; all twelve elements are vital. The only distinction is in the quantities required.

Major elements are needed by the plants in relatively large amounts whereas trace elements are, as might be guessed, only required in minute quantities; a few parts per million in fact. On the whole, fertilisers that are derived from organic sources, such as hoof and horn, fish meal, seaweed meal and treated town refuse, contain trace elements as well as major elements.

Despite the fact that most truly organic materials contain all the essential elements in varying proportions, there is nothing consistent about them as a group or even as individuals. For example, hoof and horn contains 12–14 per cent nitrogen and 1–3 per cent phosphates. Bone meal, on the other hand, contains only about 4 per cent nitrogen but 22–25 per cent phosphates. This illustrates very clearly that no single natural fertiliser contains sufficient quantities of all the elements required by the plants. It is often necessary, therefore, to use two or more of them to supply a plant with its needs. This has to be considered alongside the fact that FYM or garden compost are also being given and these contain small amounts of plant foods as well.

FERTILISERS

We've just been looking at the different sources of bulky organic matter. Let's do the same for fertilisers now and see what they contain and how much. First, though, a quick comparison between organic and inorganic fertilisers, as there must be more nonsense said and written about this than about any other aspect of gardening.

Organics usually contain less plant foods. This means that more needs to be applied but it also makes them safer to use, from the plant's angle; it's harder to give a damaging overdose, Their nutrients are normally slower to become available but are released over a longer period. They aren't always easy to buy, and they are more expensive.

Inorganics, on the other hand, are cheaper and more readily available. They contain a higher proportion of plant foods and, therefore, less needs to be applied, but they are more likely to cause damage if an overdose is given. It is much easier to make, and therefore buy, inorganic balanced feeds. They are normally quick acting.

One thing you can be sure of is that the plants can't tell any difference. All have to be broken down by the soil micro-organisms into chemicals that can be absorbed by the roots. By the time this has happened, they bear no resemblance to their original form.

Something else that is often put forward on their behalf is that organics supply the ground with organic matter. Technically, this is perfectly true but the amount that they add is minute and too small to have any significance

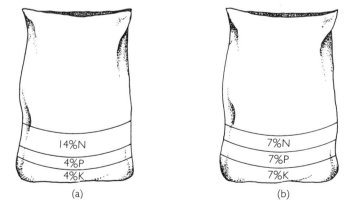
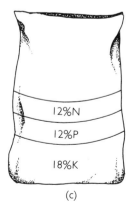

(a) 14%N 4%P 4%K

(b) 7%N 7%P 7%K

(c) 12%N 12%P 18%K

Examples of typical vegetable fertilisers, (a) High nitrogen for leafy crops, **(b)** Good general fertilizer, useful for everything, **(c)** High potash for potatoes and tomatoes.

at all. They are applied at a few ounces to the square yard. To do any good, organic matter has to be put on by the barrowful.

None of this means that I am either for or against either group of fertiliser, but 'organic freaks' tend to attribute organic fertilisers with grossly exaggerated properties. They are merely organic sources of plant nutrients; nothing more. Both types have their virtues and vices but I would be loath to bear the added cost of organics on the allegation that they are better for the plants and/or the soil. If you want to use them, by all means do but please don't run away with the idea that they have any mystical powers.

Back to the full range of fertilisers now. The conventional way in which they are classified is in terms of their N, P and K content, those elements needed in greatest amounts. The figures given below represent percentages. The fertilisers are listed alphabetically below and those designated 'O' are 'organic', in the broadest sense of the word.

The simple explanation for the large number of organic materials containing nitrogen is that it is part of the protein molecule and, as such, is found in virtually all living things. You will probably have noticed that many of the natural materials are extremely variable and this has to

	N (%)	P (%)	K (%)
ammonium nitrate	35	–	–
blood, fish and bone (O)	6	7	6
dried blood (O)	11–13	1–2	1
fish guano (O)	6–10	4–7	0.5–0.8
fish meal (O)	6	7	3
hoof and horn (O)	12–14	1–3	–
meat and bone meal (O)	6–12	1–20	–
nitrate of soda	16	–	–
nitro-chalk	15–21	–	–
poultry manure (O)	4–6	3–5	2–3
rapeseed meal (O)	5–6	1.5–3	1–1.8
soot (O)	2–11	–	–
sulphate of ammonia	21	–	–
urea	46	–	–

Nitrogen and high nitrogen fertilisers.

be taken into account when applying them. There isn't quite the same problem with 'artificials' as these are manufactured and are much more predictable.

All fertilisers offered for sale must carry in writing on the pack the percentages of the different elements. Two terms often crop up in relation to fertilisers, especially those containing nitrogen: 'slow release' and 'quick release'. These refer to the speed with which the nitrogen, or other element, is released from the fertiliser and is available to plants.

Which one is the more suitable to use will depend largely on the time of year and the crop in question. For example, fruit trees and bushes prefer a slow release form, like hoof and horn, because the nitrogen is released over a longish period

rather than all at once in a rush. Lettuces and other fast growing vegetables are better with a quick release fertiliser that gives them a boost when they need it.

Moving on to those fertilisers used for their phosphate content, phosphatic fertilisers, it will immediately be apparent from the list that there are not nearly so many to choose from. However, phosphates are not used by plants in large amounts and, being comparatively insoluble in water, they tend to remain in the soil longer than nitrogen and potash, so less needs to be applied. Often, in fact, applying phosphates every other year is perfectly adequate.

Bones are one of the main sources of organic phosphates. The table on page 48 are some of the more commonly used.

	N (%)	P (%)	K (%)
wood ash (O)	–	2–4	5–15
basic slag (O)	–	6–22	–
bone meal (O)	4	22–25	–
steamed b.m. (O)	2–4	27–30	–
fish guano (O)	6–10	4–7	0.5–0.8
fish meal (O)	8–9	9–10	1
meat and bone meal (O)	6–12	1–20	–
mineral phosphates (O)	–	25–35	–
rock phosphates (O)	–	30	–
steamed bone flour (O)	0.75–1	27–30	–
superphosphate	–	18	–
triple superphosphate	–	47	–

Phosphatic fertilisers.

Potash fertilisers are less plentiful than those high in nitrogen, but there are still several to choose from and it must not be forgotten that some of those already mentioned contain useful amounts of potassium.

One thing that all the above fertilisers have in common is that they are in a solid (dry) form. That is, they are applied to the ground dry and as they are bought. They then have to be either dissolved by rain or irrigation water or be washed into or incorporated into the soil before being converted into a form that is available to the plants. This is not always convenient, and sometimes a liquid feed is better, as with plants in containers.

Garden compost can be hung in a tub of water to produce a very useful liquid feed for plants, and this can also be done with FYM to give us manure-water (bearing in mind that the smell is not always socially acceptable when used indoors). Dried blood is fairly soluble in water and makes a good nitrogen feed when dissolved at the rate of 1 oz in 2 gallons of water. This is first-rate as a tonic for the plants. Various other concoctions and infusions have been dreamed up over the years but none seem to have any particular advantage over the more orthodox ones.

There is one material, however, that is possibly better than most others as a liquid feed – concentrated seaweed extract (Maxicrop). This is available in several formulations, some of which have man-made soluble fertilisers added to increase the strength and suitability of the product for different crops. The one described as

	N (%)	P (%)	K (%)
wood ash (O)	–	2–4	5–15
cement kiln dust (O)	–	–	5–6
flue dust (O)	–	–	trace–6
kainit (O)	–	–	14
dried kelp (O)	2.5	1.5	15
manure salts (O)	–	–	20–30
muriate of potash	–	–	40–60
potassium nitrate	12–14	–	42–44
rock potash (O)	–	–	11
sulphate of potash	–	–	48–52

Potash fertilisers.

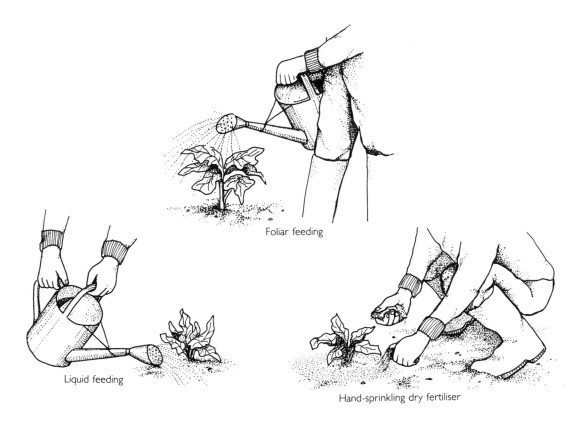

Foliar feeding

Liquid feeding

Hand-sprinkling dry fertiliser

Three ways of feeding plants.

'natural' is the pure seaweed extract with no additives.

This particular type of feed has a number of advantages, Firstly, it is a complete feed in itself; trace elements are included. Secondly, it is excellent as a foliar feed (one applied to the leaves with a watering can or sprayer) as well as a root fertiliser. Thirdly, it is equally suitable for mature plants as well as for new seedlings.

Having mentioned these three main ways of feeding plants, dry and liquid root fertilisers and foliar feeds, it's vital to look at the advantages and disadvantages of each to decide which is the best type to use for a particular job.

Dry Fertiliser

There is no doubt that dry fertilisers are the most convenient to use. All you have to do is open the pack, take out a handful and sprinkle it on the ground. If it is being applied as a base dressing before sowing or planting a crop, it would be cultivated in as a matter of course. If it is used as a top dressing, it would be hoed in.

Where the soil is dry, watering helps to speed up the fertiliser's action, otherwise you just sit back and wait for things to happen. As I have mentioned, the normal system with vegetables is to apply only a base dressing before sowing or planting to quick growing crops, like lettuces, other salads and summer cabbage, but follow this with a top dressing for those vegetables that crop for a long time. French and runner beans and peas are good examples of these.

The normal inorganic fertiliser used for both purposes and for all vegetables is Growmore. This first saw the light of day during the last war when it formed part of the 'Dig for Victory' campaign to encourage people to grow their own vegetables at home. It's still going strong and, for a general purpose fertiliser, has yet to be beaten.

The main reason for Growmore's success is its relatively low and safe (to plants) nutrient content (NPK 7:7:7) but there is ample of all three of the elements most in demand by the majority of plants. For the organically minded, Blood, Fish and Bone is the equivalent at about 6:7:6. This figure will vary from brand to brand, depending on the source and proportion of the different components. The one I've quoted is a reasonable average, but I have a pack in front of me where the analysis is 5.1:5:6.5, so you'll see that it varies.

Observant and/or experienced gardeners will realise that dry fertilisers have one important shortcoming; they need water to dissolve them so that they are in a fit state to be acted upon by the soil microorganisms before being absorbed by roots. If they remain dry after application, they are, of course, completely useless. This is a fairly rare occurrence in the UK but it does sometimes happen to top dressings in the summer.

Liquid Fertiliser

If plants need feeding during periods of drought, and many will, the answer lies in the use of a liquid feed, which serves the double purpose of supplying both water and nutrients. In addition, because the nutrients are already in a dissolved state, they have the benefit of being quickly taken up by the plants. You can make use of this virtue at other times when a rapid response is wanted, and when feeding plants in containers.

Unfortunately, liquid feeds also have a slight snag. As a direct result of being readily soluble and quickly available, they are also soon used up or washed out of the soil and need to be replaced more frequently than dry fertilisers. The speed of their disappearance is dependent on such things as the type of soil (heavy soils retain them longer) and the rainfall.

A very general recommendation for using liquid fertilisers to feed vegetables growing in the open ground would be to apply them about every three to four weeks.

Foliar Feeds

If a really quick response is wanted, a foliar feed, such as seaweed extract, should be used. The elements within these are readily absorbed by the leaves as well as by the roots and, because the material is sprayed on to the leaves, the response is almost immediate. That's a rather grand claim, but you could expect to see results in well under a week during the summer.

Incidentally, older gardeners may well remember the popularity of soot-water. This was made by hanging a bag of soot in a water butt in the same way that one does with FYM or garden compost. The resulting brew made a good foliar feed by supplying nitrogen. It also had some powers of dissuasion towards certain pests and diseases.

The important point about foliar feeding is that it should never be regarded as the main way of feeding plants. Unless you use a complete feed, like seaweed, the diet is likely to be incomplete and, besides that, it would need to be applied so frequently as to become a chore. The roots are the organs that plants use for absorbing food; keep it that way.

Foliar feeding really comes into its own when a plant is suffering, or when you want it to put in just that little bit more effort, or at a naturally stressful time, such as during the flowering period of peas and beans, when a little extra help will pay dividends. Plants that have recently been moved will derive enormous benefit from a foliar feed because it will sustain them until the roots have become established and can take over. Also, by strengthening the leaves and making them operate better, foliar feeding will encourage the roots to grow and take over all the quicker.

Those, then, are the three main ways of feeding plants, and circumstances will dictate which is best for a particular type of plant at a given moment.

Plant nutrition is an extremely complicated science, but fortunately we don't need to know the whys and wherefores of it all because Mother Nature has endowed plants with almost boundless tolerance. However, a bad gardener, or one who fails to feed his plants properly, will soon find out that there is a limit to their endurance. It is worth bearing this in mind if you like to garden 'organically' because the fertilisers involved cost a good deal more than artificials. As a result of this, there may come a time when it is felt that putting the plants on a diet to save on the cost of fertilisers will do no harm; it most certainly will.

As an essentially practical book about growing vegetables, I have kept theoretical horticulture to a minimum. However, no account of plant nutrition would be complete without a look at the biochemical world of what part the most important elements play within the plant. Understanding a little of this helps the gardener appreciate which elements are the most important for a given crop, and why. This, in turn, will make it possible for you to buy a more specialised fertiliser if needed.

Nitrogen, the first to be considered, is used for leaf and heart production, as in lettuces and cabbages; it gives bulk and size to a plant and the rich green colour we all associate with a healthy and well-fed vegetable. Also, it is part of the protein molecule found in all cells and, therefore, a shortage will lead to smaller cells, and thus smaller plants.

As part of the chlorophyll molecule, a shortage of nitrogen will also lead to pale leaves and therefore, again, smaller and less productive plants.

Phosphates are important for good root development, quick establishment, early maturity and the ripening of seeds and fruits. A shortage will slow down cell division at the growing points, and hence slow down growth. Phosphates also help with photosynthesis and disease resistance.

Potash encourages balanced growth, by reducing the effect of nitrogen, and improves the quality of fruit and flowers. It also gives better frost and disease resistance. Potash is another element that plays a part in photosynthesis (the conversion of gaseous carbon dioxide into solid carbohydrates) and therefore a shortage will, again, slow down growth.

Calcium plays an important part in the growth process by being a major constituent of the walls of individual cells. A shortage will lead to a reduction in cell formation and diminished root systems with reduced mineral uptake.

Calcium, in the form of chalk and lime, will reduce soil acidity and will make heavy soils easier to cultivate by drawing together the tiny particles into crumbs and blocks, thus giving the soil a better structure.

Magnesium is yet another part of the chlorophyll molecule, with all that implies. Anyone who has grown tomatoes will probably know what a shortage looks like; a yellowing between the veins of the older leaves and, therefore, reduced cropping as well as slower growth.

The only other element you are really likely to have any dealings with is iron. However, it's very seldom that vegetables suffer from a shortage; the usual victims are ericaceous plants (rhododendrons and azaleas) growing on a chalky soil. Luckily, vegetables are remarkably free from this sort of trouble.

The latest thing in plant nutrition is a product called 'Pea and Bean Booster'. This is an inoculum of the naturally-occurring bacterium *Rhizobium* that is found in the root nodules of all peas and beans. This bacterium 'fixes' the raw materials for making nitrogen for the host plant to feed on. Thus the nitrogen-fixing bacteria are in the soil, around the roots, right from the word go. It really does give the crops a kick-start and I wouldn't mind betting that other similar products will follow.

GARDEN COMPOST

Before leaving the underground part of vegetable gardening, garden compost must be looked at in more detail. Having come to the conclusion that ordinary garden compost is as good as any source of bulky organic matter, and cheaper, the gardener must learn how to make good garden compost.

Incidentally, the type of compost we are talking about here is the properly rotted waste vegetation from the garden and home; it should not be confused with seed and potting composts. These are special materials, in which seeds are sown and plants grown in containers of one sort or another.

The kind of compost I am concerned with here, garden compost, is the kind you put into the garden. It can consist of any or all of the following materials: lawn mowings, weeds, hedge clippings, spent vegetable plants, dead flowers, leaves of all sorts, soft prunings, sawdust, wood shavings, wood ashes, straw and hay, pet droppings and animal manures. To this list can be added household waste such as cabbage leaves, vegetable peelings, tea leaves, egg shells and even the contents of vacuum cleaners.

More or less anything of vegetative origin can be used to make garden compost. When discussing garden compost, I am referring to the decayed or decaying remains of these materials. What is called 'well rotted' compost is a dark brown, rich material that is fairly dry and which easily breaks up in the hand.

Woody materials, such as thick hedge clippings and prunings, take a long time to decompose but will, eventually, provide the most humus, humus mainly being derived from the lignin in woody material. As long as twigs and the like are chopped up into small pieces with a shredder or something similar, they can be a valuable raw material but are still best mixed with softer tissues. If large prunings and bits of wood are available, they should first be burnt and the ashes added to the compost heap or bin.

Newspaper in small amounts, such as from the bottom of pets' cages, is splendid, especially if shredded, but large quantities must be avoided. Not only does it take a

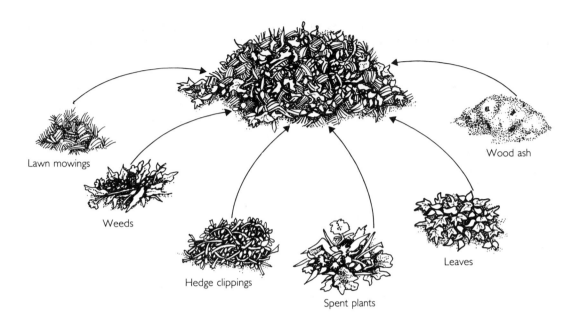

Lawn mowings

Weeds

Hedge clippings

Spent plants

Leaves

Wood ash

Some of the most readily available raw materials for turning into garden compost.

long time to rot down, it is also of little, if any, value to the soil.

There are very few things of organic origin that cannot be turned into compost but it should be remembered that some materials are only suitable in small amounts. We have already mentioned newspaper but too many evergreen leaves or pine needles also take a long time to break down and become usable. The roots of perennial weeds, such as docks, thistles and ground elder, must be dried and killed before composting them; alternatively, they should be burnt or put in the garden waste recycling bin.

Rhubarb leaves are often said to be bad for a compost heap, but they are perfectly safe in what might be called domestic quantities. It is when large amounts are put in over the course of weeks that trouble might arise. There's nothing mysterious about them except that they contain an extraordinarily large amount of oxalic acid.

Anything which gives rise to acidic conditions is bad because decomposition occurs best in a neutral or alkaline environment.

Plants infested or infected by pests and diseases are also frowned upon by many gardeners but most are destroyed either by the heat generated in the heap or by the very fact that they are in a hostile environment for a considerable time. Some *are* best avoided, though. These are the soil-borne ones and the victims of such things as club root disease, cabbage root fly and carrot fly should not be put in a compost heap.

Lawn mowings are perfectly suitable for composting – in fact they often form the backbone of the heap in summer. However, they are much better if mixed with other and coarser things first. In a thick layer, they are apt to lie cold and soggy after the initial heat generation.

Another point to bear in mind about mowings concerns those that come from a lawn that has been treated with a selective weedkiller. If the treatment took place from April to the end of July, the mowings can be added to the compost heap and it will be quite safe to use the compost in the autumn. If, though, the treatment was after July, then it is safer to leave the compost until the spring just in case it still contains traces of the weedkiller. This is worth mentioning because many gardeners beg, borrow or steal raw material for their compost heaps with little knowledge of its history.

On the subject of lawn weedkillers, it used to be quite common practice to grow tomatoes in partially decomposed straw bales. This is still fine in principle but it must only be done if you can be sure that the corn crop from which the straw came was not treated with a hormone-type weedkiller before it was harvested; these contain the same chemicals as lawn weedkillers. Tomatoes are particularly sensitive to these weedkillers and will be damaged by them if applied in your compost.

To return to composting; the greater variety there is in a heap, the better the resulting compost will be. A mixture of firm and soft materials will give good results.

Having looked at the sort of things that can and cannot be put in the compost heap, it would be helpful to know how compost is formed so that the knowledge can be used to your advantage. The decomposition of waste vegetation is carried out by beneficial micro-organisms, which need air (oxygen) and moisture to survive and operate efficiently. The amount of air and moisture required, whilst not being critical, is important, in that too much air will lead to the raw materials drying out whilst too little will encourage the wrong type of microbe.

Too much moisture will force out a lot of the air and thereby reduce the microbe population. At the same time, it will discourage the build-up of heat within the heap. Too little moisture will cause the whole process to grind to a halt.

A good supply of nitrogen is also essential as this forms an important part of the diet of the micro-organisms. Whilst a certain amount is provided by the plants' remains, the whole composting process is greatly speeded up if extra is added. Nitrogen used for this purpose is referred to as an 'activator' or 'accelerator' and there is one particular proprietary product, Garotta, which is available in all gardening retailers.

Given a correctly built heap made with the right material, decomposition will occur by itself; the use of an accelerator simply hastens the process and makes it more complete. This speeding up may not seem particularly important but it means that more heat is generated during decomposition and this is vital if weed seeds and other undesirables in the heap are to be destroyed.

The word 'heap' keeps cropping up in relation to composting and this is certainly the traditional way of making compost. However, there are heaps and there are heaps, and an untidy heap is an abomination, whether it be large or small.

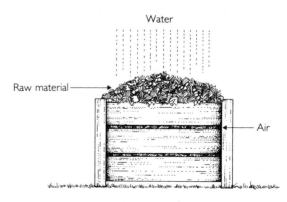

The three essentials for good garden compost.

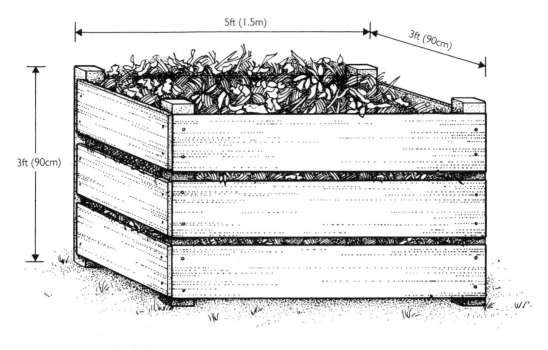

5ft (1.5m)

3ft (90cm)

3ft (90cm)

Model for a home-made compost heap. Corrugated iron could be used in place of planks.

Anything that looks like a pile of garden rubbish thrown into a corner is likely to produce correspondingly awful compost, as well as creating a general air of slovenliness. Before we start making compost, therefore, there are several questions that have to be answered concerning the type of heap, or other container, that is going to be most convenient for us. Firstly, how much raw material is likely to be available? Secondly, how much compost is going to be needed? And finally, is the compost going to be required all at once or as a steady supply throughout the year?

If there is only a small amount of raw material or the need for compost is strictly limited, then a small heap or, better still, a ready-made composting bin, is usually the answer.

On the other hand, if waste vegetation is plentiful and all the compost that can be produced is used, then one or more large heaps would be more sensible. This would also be the best system where compost is only needed once a year for, say, digging in during the autumn.

If, though, compost is going to be wanted for various jobs throughout the year, it would be wiser to have a number of bins or small heaps with compost maturing on a sort of production line.

Where it has been decided that bins are inappropriate, the question arises as to what is the best way of containing a heap so that it looks tidy and operates effectively. The heap should be as near round or square as is convenient, to encourage the quickest and most even decomposition. The width should be not much more than 4–5ft (1.2–1.5m) but the length can be up to about 6ft (1.8m). The width is the important measurement because, with a wider heap, air will have difficulty in penetrating to the centre. For the same reason, 3–4ft (0.9–1.2m) would be about the maximum desirable height.

The ideal site for such a heap would be in the angle of a fence or wall, where two sides are already provided. In this case it is better to put a sheet of tin or something similar against the fence or wall to prevent its deterioration or the bridging of any damp-course. The other two sides can be made of corrugated iron with holes driven through, or planks nailed 1cm apart to upright supports.

Wood is generally considered superior to corrugated iron, not only because it looks better but also because it provides better insulation against the cold in winter.

If you decide to have a bin as opposed to a heap there are several models to choose from, or you can even make your own. Bins which incorporate perforated polythene sheeting or which are made of more substantial plastic, wood or even bricks all have the advantage of retaining heat and moisture quite well in spite of the small volume.

Purpose-made compost bins are ideal for small gardens.

The one proviso is that the bin should have a top, as this will not only keep the heat and moisture in but will also prevent too much rain getting in. Nor is the necessity for a top confined to bins; traditional heaps also operate far better when covered.

The size of compost bins varies but they're somewhat bigger than a large dustbin. Their shape, material and effectiveness are about as variable as their price.

Unfortunately, the high price of some models has deterred many newcomers to gardening from even setting foot on the composting ladder; they assume that all other aspects of the job are equally as expensive. This is absolutely wrong and the makers of highly priced but poor bins are doing neither themselves nor the gardeners any good at all. I have to include most rotating bins here; they're far too expensive for what benefits they may have.

If you fancy having a go at making your own bin, very good results can be had from old dustbins with the bottoms knocked out and some holes punched in the side; and the original lid makes an excellent cover.

Another approach is to make a wire netting cylinder 3–4ft (0.9–1.2m) high and not less than about 30in (75cm) across. This is supported by canes woven through the netting and a bottomless dustbin bag is placed inside to enclose the compost. It looks a bit Heath Robinson, or rough and ready, but works admirably and costs very little. Heaps and bins smaller than this are not a good idea, as insufficient heat is generated and retained.

Having set the scene, the time has come to start composting. Most gardens produce a range of useful materials and, for the best results, these should be mixed together, building the heap up in layers.

If an accelerator is being used, this should be added every 6in (15cm) or so.

Try to mix dry and wet materials together so that the moisture content is reasonably even. If anything is really dry, it should be thoroughly soaked before it is added to the heap.

A careful firming of the heap or bin is needed when fairly woody materials are in use in order to exclude large air pockets. If the heap appears to be drying out in the summer, it is perfectly in order to wet it so that activity is maintained. This should not be overdone, or excessive cooling may take place.

In the past, and before the days of effective accelerators, it was common practice to build up a compost heap in the course of one year, turn it inside-out and upside-down and leave it for another year. This ensured that it was completely and evenly rotted and in a fit state to use. If an accelerator and a good heap or bin are used, this is not usually needed.

When a heap or bin is complete and has been properly made, cover it and leave it to decompose. This will start very quickly. The time taken for compost to become sufficiently decomposed and usable will vary enormously. The biggest variables are the nature of the raw materials and the time of year.

If soft material is being composted in the summer, it can be fully decomposed in about two months. On the other hand, chopped up prunings put on in the late autumn are unlikely to be fit for at least six months or even a year.

One of the slowest materials to decompose is autumn leaves. In reasonable amounts, these can be mixed in with the other vegetation to be composted but, if there are a lot, it is best to deal with them on their own, and the addition of an activator is a great help. Also, make sure it stays moist.

The formation of good leafmould usually takes at least a year but this will vary with the type of leaves. Beech and oak are two of the quickest to rot down but plane, sycamore and horse chestnut take a lot longer because of their thick veins and stalks.

Some people recommend adding layers of soil to a heap to provide additional micro-organisms. Although the introduction of soil in the natural course of events, such as on plant roots, is quite in order, the deliberate formation of layers of soil can seriously interfere with the composting process by creating cold layers in which no decomposition occurs at all.

We discussed the situation as regards lawn mowings and those treated with weed-killer, but lawn rakings are another valuable source of material for composting. These are perfectly safe, even if they do contain a high proportion of moss. Although this may not rot down completely, there is no risk of any moss establishing itself in other parts of the garden when the compost is finally used.

If it is anticipated that a particular batch of material is going to be reluctant to break down, the addition of an activator immediately above it normally puts matters right. There are, of course, occasions when a lot of the same material turns up all at once; autumn leaves are a good example. Evergreen leaves and pine needles are best added to the normal mixed compost heap because, on their own, they can take years to rot down. No leaves need be rejected; they all make good compost if treated correctly – it's just that some take longer to decompose than others. All leaves should have plenty of water when being composted.

Sawdust is tricky stuff, but also very valuable if dealt with properly. Its woody nature makes it an excellent raw material for humus. It does, however, take a long time to break down. In small amounts it can safely be added to the general heap but, if a lot is available, it is best composted separately in much the same way as leaves. The other answer is to build the heap with thoroughly wet sawdust and mix in the activator as the heap is being made.

We've already seen that small amounts of straw can be mixed with grass mowings and added to the heap. The grass will then make better compost and the straw will break down quicker. Large amounts, however, are best composted alone. There are several ways of doing it, all of which benefit from an activator being included:

1   By watering the straw and layering it with green and sodden material.
2   By only watering it.
3   As in 1, but not watering it and allowing the rain to provide the moisture. This takes the longest of all.

When composting straw, make sure that it is thoroughly loose and always stack it high rather than wide – it decomposes much more quickly.

One of the best ways to decompose straw is to build a sort of stockade of bales and fill up the middle with loose straw. This keeps the heap tidy and allows it to decompose right up to the edges. Tread the whole thing down when completed and give it a thorough soaking.

The retaining wall need not be bales – planks or boards are just as good if held in place with stakes. The advantage of using bales, though, is that, when the composting of one batch is finished, those used for the wall will be half rotted themselves and can be shaken out for the next batch of compost, whilst fresh bales are used for the new walls. As a rough guide, two tons of dry straw will need a heap about 9ft (2.7m) square whilst 6–10 tons will need about 18ft (5.4m) square.

If materials other than straw are included in the heap, spread them out evenly. Tread the heap down as before and give it enough water to soak it thoroughly. A heap can perfectly well be built without walls but it is not as efficient and, of course, the straw does not rot right down to the edges.

In some parts of the country, raw materials like bracken and seaweed are in plentiful supply and these make particularly good compost. Bracken contains a lot of potash and is best treated like straw.

We have discussed the virtues of seaweed already but, for composting, it should first be allowed to drain to get rid of most of the salt. The best system is then to mix it with straw before composting it. Normally, no activator is needed because of the readily available nitrogen it contains.

If a lot of annual weeds are going to be put on a compost heap there is always a danger that any seeds they are carrying will simply be distributed when the finished compost is spread. The obvious way of avoiding this is to 'harvest' the weeds before they come into flower but, should this not happen, flowering and seeding weeds should be put in the centre of the heap and then covered with other material to stop them growing and releasing mature seed. The greatest heat is also produced in the middle and it should kill the seeds.

Covering all live weeds is particularly important in the winter when they are apt to stay alive, even when uprooted, in the cool and damp conditions that are found on top of the heap.

Something that falls quite neatly into the category of composting is the use of turf to form the basis of the other kind of compost; seed and potting mixtures for growing plants in. If you are making your own John Innes-type of compost, you will need a good supply of fibrous loam. One of the best sources of this is old grassland. Start by stripping the turves off so that there is about 5cm (2in) of soil below the grass.

Lay the turves on the ground, grass side up, and put the next layer on them grass side down to form a sort of grass sandwich. Carry on building like this until all the turves have gone. If you want to hasten the death of the grass and its decomposition, sprinkle some activator into the middle of each 'sandwich'.

USING GARDEN COMPOST

Well-rotted garden compost certainly does work wonders; all plants derive enormous benefit from the improving effect that it has on the soil. Having looked at its manufacture, therefore, what are we to do with it once it is ready for the garden?

There are four main ways in which it can be used. The most common, and probably the one that springs immediately to mind, is digging it into the soil to a depth of about 1ft (30cm) to improve the structure and to add to the plant foods already there. The normal, yet quite wrong, method of doing this is to dig out the first trench on the plot, spread the compost in the bottom of it and then turn the next lot over on to it.

Why this is quite wrong is because the compost is buried out of sight and completely out of reach of young plants' roots. The plant has to be well-established and growing strongly before it can reach and benefit from the compost. This destroys the whole object of the exercise, which is to help plants to grow from the moment they are put in the ground. Clearly, therefore, the compost has to be spread through as great a depth of soil as possible.

The way to achieve this is not to throw it into the bottom of the trench but to spread it in front of you over the face of the trench so that the full depth of soil benefits. Only in that way will the plants be helped immediately they germinate or are planted. There is also a right and a wrong way of doing the actual digging; we will be looking at that later.

Another common use for garden compost is as a mulch instead of peat or bark. For anyone new to gardening, this is the practice of covering the ground between plants with a layer of organic material 4–6in (10–15cm) deep. This has a number

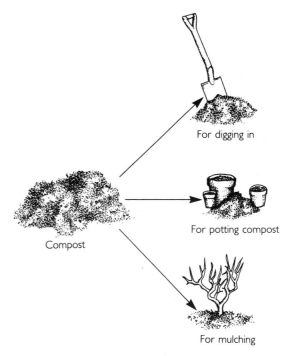

For digging in

For potting compost

For mulching

Compost

Some of the more popular uses for garden compost.

of beneficial effects. Firstly, it helps to prevent the soil from drying out and capping in the summer. The compost forms a blanket on the soil surface so that much less water is lost by evaporation. For this reason, it should be obvious that the mulch must be put down at a time when the ground is thoroughly moist. If it goes on when the ground is dry, it simply acts as a mackintosh and stops any rain from soaking in. April is a good time to mulch.

Mulching will also help to keep the weeds down. Weed seeds operate in the same way as any other seeds do – they have to be near the surface to germinate and grow properly. Unfortunately, mulching does not affect established perennial weeds; they have to be killed by other means.

The other important job performed by a mulch is, hardly surprisingly, the addition of organic matter to the soil. Apart from digging it in and using it as a mulch, garden compost can be used in the making of seed and potting composts. Here we come to a big snag – weeds, again. Unless the compost is particularly well rotted or great care has been taken to exclude weed seeds, the most awful mess can result. Weeds will spring up everywhere and the proper seeds will be smothered in the resulting forest. One way round this is to heat-sterilise the seed or potting compost after it has been made, rather than just the loam.

On the whole, it is wiser not to rely on home-made seed and potting composts but to buy proprietary ones. When you are spending quite a lot of money on seeds, the possible saving in the cost of compost is too high a price to pay on the off-chance that things will turn out satisfactorily – they seldom do.

For preparing your own liquid plant food, however, there is little better than well-rotted garden compost. FYM has been

used for this purpose for years, so why not compost; the nutrient values are similar?

The process is exactly the same as for manure-water in that a bag of garden compost is hung in a water tub so that the goodness seeps into the water. This is then used to feed plants. There are no weeds, no pests, no diseases and, unlike manure-water, no smell – well, not as much!

The process is that some sacking is filled with well-rotted compost and tied at the top. The whole thing is then sunk into a container of water, preferably rainwater. Make sure, if possible, that the sacking is tied to something outside the container. If a 40 gallon drum is used it can present difficulties when you want to retrieve the bag if you simply dropped it in.

In about a week, the liquid should be ready to use. The way to work out how much compost to use is to allow about 1lb (½kg) for every gallon (4½ litres) of water. No dilution is required when the infusion is drawn off. When any liquid is taken out, top up the container with more water. A bag of compost should last for 5–6 weeks, after which time most of the nutrients will have gone and a fresh start will have to be made. The spent compost can be used on the garden.

Before leaving the subject of garden compost and composting, it would be worthwhile having a quick look at one or two materials that are available for improving the soil, some of which purport to do away with the need for bulky organic matter. Probably the most readily available is ground-calcified seaweed. This is a perfectly natural material and is derived from a seaweed that is more like a coral than a plant. It has a very high calcium carbonate content and, as such, a high pH as well. In all honesty, it is an expensive way of buying chalk or limestone but it does have the advantage of containing trace elements. It is used in the same way as lime in that it is applied to the ground after digging, when it helps to create a good tilth for sowing or planting in.

Another form of seaweed that is of more value in improving the soil is also a completely natural material. It is what we think of as normal seaweed that has been harvested, composted and ground up. This also has the trace elements but by far its greatest virtue is that it is rich in alginates, the material mentioned earlier as being first rate at improving the structure of all soils be they heavy, medium or light.

Both these products are natural, genuine and work, within limits. Neither profess to do away with the need for bulky organic matter but certainly the composted seaweed is a great help in creating a good tilth. As the manufacturers say, it speeds up what nature takes rather a long time to do if left to itself.

There are a number of other so-called 'soil conditioners' on the market but most are of purely chemical origin and have no lasting effect.

SHREDDERS

As a final word on composting, we must not forget shredders. There are two kinds – noisy ones and quiet ones; I have owned both. However, for the last five years or so I have had a quiet one and I would't be without it for the world. Shredders make a smashing job of breaking up bits of vegetation (thick roots, small branches, etc.) that are far too big to put into the compost heap without grinding them up.

Where bins are being used, shredders are useful because they chop up everything into the sort of size that will decompose in reasonable time. Obviously there is no point in putting soft vegetation through a shredder but, for chopping up all manner of prunings, brassica stalks, thick hedge clippings, the tougher flower stems and even newspaper, they're well worth using as virtually nothing of vegetative origin need be wasted.

A good shredder will make short work even of branches up to I in (2–3cm) across. Do, though, get a powered model; hand cranked ones are very hard work and not awfully effective. Remember, though, that the more woody material you put into a heap or bin, the more need there is for an activator.

A good shredder can be a bit pricey but, if there is a lot of work for it to do or if the cost can be shared with a friend, it is well worth considering.

A word of warning to finish off with, though, and this applies to all sectors of gardening. Every gardener should guard against becoming over-mechanised. Not only can machines be expensive and noisy things but they also have the annoying habit of going wrong at the critical moment and also of needing either electricity or petrol to operate them. Consider carefully, therefore, if a particular machine is really worth having before you commit yourself.

6 Watering

The natural companion to feeding plants is, surely, watering them. Of the two, watering is certainly the more important; a plant can live for quite a long time without food, but can be dead after a couple of days without water. This isn't very surprising when you consider that about 75 per cent of the weight of a living plant is water.

There used to be a belief, there may still be, that once you start watering the garden, you have to carry on until there's a really good downpour. This is a time-honoured tradition often perpetuated by older gardeners. It's nonsense and yet, like so many of these old beliefs and sayings, there's a grain of truth in it; or rather, it can frequently be based on a half-truth.

The normal drill for a new gardener, when they see that things are getting parched, is to go out into the garden with a watering-can and make it go as far as possible. This usually results in the water soaking in an inch or two at the very most; usually it just lays the dust.

Under dry soil conditions, plants tend to put out new roots into the soil which is the moistest. Under the above watering conditions, this is on the surface – and it is this surface layer which is the first to dry out when the sun comes out again. Unfortunately, this is the layer where all the young roots are and, without water, they'll simply shrivel up. You therefore have to keep on watering to ensure that this

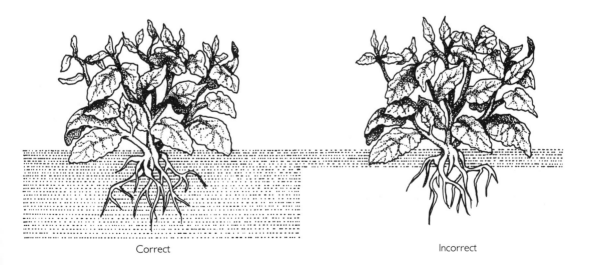

Correct   Incorrect

Correct watering ensures that a good depth of soil is thoroughly wetted.

surface soil remains moist Hence the origin of the belief.

If you water properly, however, and give enough for it to soak down a good 6in (15cm) or so, the problem won't arise because the roots won't be duped into growing only near the surface in the damp earth. Also, the soil will stay damp for much longer and, even in the driest conditions, you could well get away with watering only about once a week instead of every day.

Incidentally, the idea that it's best to water in the evening as opposed to the morning is largely correct. It's much cooler at night and the plants are under far less stress. This means that they'll be able to take their time absorbing water and, by the morning, will have taken up all they can hold. Also, the water will have a chance to soak down into the soil and won't just evaporate the moment it hits the soil.

TIMING AND QUANTITY

Quite a lot is known about the water needs of vegetables as, being an economic food crop, a lot of research has gone into it. Not only do we know how much water a particular crop needs but we also know the times during its life when water is most important and when a shortage is going to be most damaging.

Here are a few examples. Peas and beans need plenty of water when they're flowering and again when the pods are swelling. Root crops, such as carrots, turnips, radishes and parsnips, need a steady supply throughout their life to maintain even growth. If water is available in fits and starts, it simply leads to surges of growth and the inevitable splitting of the root. Much the same applies to tomatoes.

With potatoes, a thorough soaking when the young tubers are about the size of marbles is the most beneficial, though here again they should never be allowed to run short. If they are, growth will stop temporarily and, after a soaking, it will start again. This doesn't always lead to splitting but to a phenomenon known as 'second growth' when lumps and bumps and odd protuberances grow out from the tubers. Grand for children to make animals from but pretty useless as vegetables. Plenty of water for early potatoes also means that they can often be lifted earlier, when they are at their most expensive to buy.

Brassicas, celery and other 'green' vegetables, such as lettuces, usually have a critical time in the last couple of weeks or so before they're ready to be gathered. Keep them well watered then.

Radishes, summer turnips and kohl rabi should always be grown fast with plenty of feed and water or they'll go woody; radishes will often bolt as well (send up a flower stem).

If summer and autumn cauliflowers get any more than a slight check to their development, it invariably leads to the curds bursting and running up to flowers when they are still quite small. Calabrese is the same.

On the whole, there isn't a single vegetable that actually likes to run short of water; the best that can be said is that some will tolerate it better than others. By the same token, none like to be waterlogged for any length of time either.

The next point we have to consider is the amount of water that should be given at any one time. We've seen that 'a little and often' is worse than a waste of time because it does the plants more harm than good. Washing them out of the ground is equally bad.

A flourishing allotment garden full of vegetables of all kinds.

Double digging – manure has been spread along the trench.

French beans intercropped with lettuce.

'Ishiko' – a modern Japanese salad onion.

Red 'Salad Bowl' lettuce.

BELOW: Green 'Salad Bowl' lettuce.

'Lollo Rossa' lettuces.

'Meteor Vroma' broad beans.

'Aquadulce' broad beans.

'Sungold' tomatoes growing in a greenhouse.

'Bright Lights' chard.

Purple sprouting broccoli.

'Ajax' Brussels
sprouts.

BELOW: 'White Rock'
cauliflower.

A beautiful crop of freshly-dug new potatoes.

Chitting potatoes.

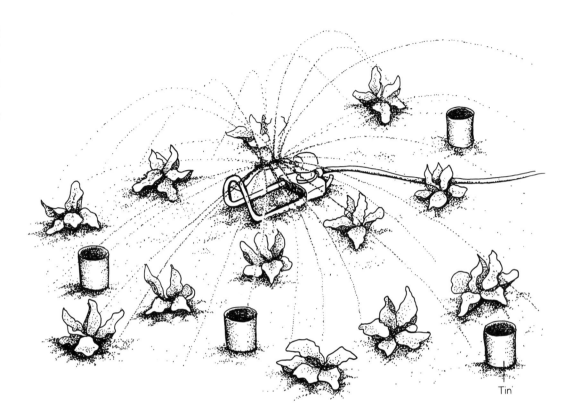

Tin

A simple way of measuring the amount of water applied to an area.

When you water, give at least half an inch (1.5cm) and preferably an inch (2.5cm). If you're using a sprinkler, this is easy enough to measure. Stand a few empty tins on the area being watered and measure the water that collects in them until it's reached the amount you want. If you can guarantee turning on the tap to the same point every time, you can see how long it takes to deliver the required amount and make a note of it for next time. You have to be fairly accurate though.

A much better way is to attach a water meter to the tap and run the hose from that. Don't worry, these can be bought for a reasonable price. It will measure out any quantity you like from about 15 to 420 gallons simply by the turning of a dial. When the set amount has been delivered, it automatically cuts off the supply – couldn't be easier.

Small areas, such as single rows and the like, can either be watered with a handheld hose with a rose on the end, or a watering can. With the hose it isn't always easy to judge the amount of water you have given, but with a can you'll be able to work it out on the basis of 1 in of water for 1 sq.yd being about 13 pints.

Here are a couple of other useful figures: 1 in over 50 sq.yd is roughly 230 gallons. Four gallons per sq.yd are needed to soak 1ft deep into medium loam.

METHODS OF WATERING

We then have to tackle the question of how best the water should be applied to a particular area. This may sound easy enough but don't forget that most vegetable plots are based on the square or the rectangular. Many sprinklers, on the other hand, water circular areas.

It's not all gloom, though, because most of the oscillating types (rather than those that spin) and all the perforated hose sorts can water square or rectangular pieces of land.

First, though, let's have a look at the different types of gadget available, and how to tell the good from the bad and the indifferent. It isn't so much the type or design of the sprinkler that can be good or bad, these are fairly standard; it's the brand or make that can let you down.

There are three basic designs for gardens; the rotary sprinkler, the oscillating sprinkler and the sprinkler (perforated) hose. Rotary sprinklers are the sort that spin round because of the pressure of the water going through them, and they cover circular areas. The cheapest, which are often perfectly adequate, are pushed into the ground and work by jets of water striking a star-shaped disc. This breaks up the jets into droplets. They are suitable for areas up to about 25ft (7½m) across.

Larger and slightly more sophisticated are the sprinklers with a spinning head, from which the water is thrown out through two or three nozzles. Some have adjustable nozzles so that the droplet size can be altered. These will treat circular areas up to 40–50ft (12–15m) across.

Oscillating sprinklers are the ones used for watering square or rectangular plots. The head consists of a pipe bent into an arch with nozzle holes in it. Water pressure moves the head from one side to the other in a semi-circle. The better ones are adjustable to cover many shapes and areas.

In its simplest form, the sprinkler hose is a length of hose, oval in section, with tiny holes on one side. There are two ways of using it, either with the holes facing upward so that the water is thrown out in fine jets, or with the holes next to the ground. In the latter case, less water pressure is used and the water trickles out of the holes to irrigate just a narrow strip of ground, such as a row of seeds or seedlings.

Sprinklers used to be made of brass or, more recently, cast alloy. Nowadays, they're usually plastic but with some of the better makes having metal nozzles. Plastic, of course, is not going to corrode but is much lighter. This has led to some of the better manufacturers compensating for the lack of weight by causing the machine to fill up with water before it starts to discharge; this makes it heavy enough to remain stable and in one place when the water is running. With the cheaper models, you may have to pin them to the ground. It's probably as well to find this out before you buy.

Possibly the most up-to-date watering device is what might be called a 'dial-a-pattern'. Simply by turning the disc which contains the nozzles, a different shape or size of pattern of cover can be selected. Make sure you buy a well-known make, though, as there are some rather shoddy ones which don't work too well.

Hoses may not appear to be a very exciting subject, but enormous strides have been made in the last ten years or so in improving their quality and standard of performance. Hoses of the past were nearly always made of rubber, the best ones made in several layers with a strengthening network of material. These have all but disappeared now, mainly because of their cost.

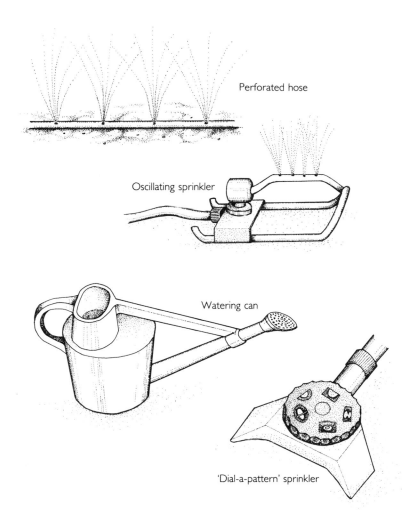

Perforated hose

Oscillating sprinkler

Watering can

'Dial-a-pattern' sprinkler

Watering devices.

They were largely replaced by the most frightful plastic things that kinked at every turn and which were completely useless when it was cold, or even cool. Now we're getting back to old standards with a few hoses being made along the same lines as the original flexible rubber ones. Instead of rubber, though, the're made of layers of supple plastic and a new type of woven nylon strengthening.

Hoses don't have to be thrown in a heap in a corner any more; we have hose reels that can be connected to the tap so that the hoses can be kept reeled on to them with water still able to run through them. This is a great advance because it means that you don't have to unreel the whole thing before connecting one end to the mains; it can be left reeled up and still work.

Another kind of hose is made along the same lines as a fireman's but obviously very much smaller, and with a polythene liner. This is rolled up flat on to a reel so that a 40ft (12m) hose will reel up to less than about 1ft (30cm) across.

WATER SOURCES

Having looked at how much water to apply with what and when, it's time to look at the different sources of water. Here again, there may be one or two you hadn't thought of. The first and most obvious is a tap and, if you haven't already got an outside one, it's certainly worth having one installed. It saves all that messing about with the tap in the sink and getting water all over the kitchen floor.

The most convenient size is a half-inch one (1cm) with a thread on it for attaching a hose. Outside taps must have a stopcock indoors so that they can be turned off and drained before the winter to avoid the risk of freeze-up and burst.

Some people feel that tap-water isn't especially good for plants and it certainly seems as though they look a lot better after a good downpour of rain. This, though, is probably as a result of the damp atmosphere that is created after a good fall of rain rather than the source of the water. However, there's one important instance when tap-water *is* unsuitable, and that is when 'hard' (chalky) water *is* used on ericaceous plants (azaleas and rhododendrons). As far as vegetables are concerned, though, don't worry as one kind of water is usually as good as another.

One snag about relying on rain-water for vegetables is that there's seldom enough available, hard though it may be to believe.

There are many other places where water can be found; they include ponds, wells, streams and rivers, even running ditches. All are perfectly satisfactory for use in the garden, provided that the water isn't contaminated. They are all more or less orthodox sources of water but, in emergencies, the list can be extended to include the apparently ridiculous. Bathwater is fine and has saved the life of many a plant during a long, hot summer. The rinsing water from a washing machine is also usable. Neither could be called ideal but they're both water and the plants won't worry about slight impurities.

WATER CONSERVATION

That completes the nuts and bolts of watering plants but there's still another topic well worth looking at – water conservation. This is becoming increasingly important with the explosion in the number of water consumers and, let's face it, the downright waste that one often sees going on in industry. Water is a commodity and has a value, but you wouldn't think so to see the way it's sometimes used.

On occasions, watering the garden becomes essential but a lot can be done to make better use of the water that is already in the soil. First of all, there are soil cultivations. As we've seen, if roots are able to penetrate deeply they are far better able to reach the cool and moist soil that lies beneath them. This is made possible by keeping the soil open, by one means or another. Occasional double digging and plenty of bulky organic matter are the main ways. Then there is the natural action of organic matter in the soil. If this is kept at a high level by the regular addition of garden compost, the water holding capacity of a sandy soil will be greatly increased.

Another good way of conserving moisture is by putting down a good, thick

3–4in (8–10cm) mulch of compost, peat or bark between standing plants. This will help enormously in preventing evaporation at the surface. It must, however, be applied when the soil is already moist or it will simply act as a mackintosh and actually prevent rain reaching the soil, making you worse off than before.

Black polythene is also a good mulch, in that it prevents evaporation and suppresses weeds; but it doesn't add organic matter to the soil, as the previous kinds do.

Incidentally, the belief that shallow surface hoeing helps in water conservation by creating a 'dust mulch' doesn't really hold water, if you'll excuse the pun. A firm surface is better because it allows a fuller root-run for the plants and enables the very important surface roots to make use of every available cubic inch of soil in their search for water. On the plus side, hoeing is definitely a good practice when it is directed at weed control; weeds will use more water than is lost by shallow hoeing.

Planting firmly and keeping the soil well consolidated will do a great deal of good, especially on light land. Something else we can do is keep the garden well sheltered from strong winds. No matter what direction they come from, winds will dry out the plants and the soil surface quicker than pretty well anything else.

Vegetables sown or planted in the autumn are far less likely to succumb to drought the following summer because they will be well established and many will be approaching maturity by the time the danger period is on them in the early summer.

It may sound odd but corrrect watering can actually save water. For example, we have already seen that evening watering allows the water to soak right down into the soil whereas, with midday watering, a fair amount of it will be evaporated.

Watering seeds and seedlings with a watering can is much more economical than with a sprinkler, and frequently it does more good.

Although water is vital, we can do a lot to reduce the amount we have to administer simply by using it wisely and economically and by ensuring that none is wasted.

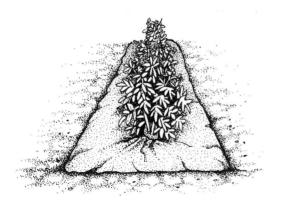

Planting potatoes through black polythene avoids the need for earthing up, suppresses weeds and conserves moisture.

7 Making a Start

One of the most frightening things for a first-time gardener to be faced with is what might be called the 'virgin' plot. It used to be possible to say that the most common one was the neglected garden but, what with all the houses shooting up these days, it's just as normal to find the virgin plot consisting of little more than a building site.

It doesn't really matter which one you're confronted by, both are equally daunting to the newcomer. Both are also dealt with in more or less the same way. The first job is to get rid of any junk and rubble that is cluttering the place up. In an established garden, this is usually in the form of broken and rusty tools, possibly a pram or bits of a bicycle and, frequently, corrugated iron. It's amazing where all this corrugated iron comes from.

If your house is newly built and was one of the first on the plot, all well and good. If, though, it was the last, you're likely to be in trouble. The simple reason for this is that builders tend to move their rubble and bits and pieces along with them from one house to the next. When they reach the end and leave the site, anything they don't want is normally left where it is; and that's usually on the last plot.

The sort of junk you're likely to find will probably be of two kinds. Firstly there will be the old paint tins, various bits of broken tackle and other metal. Secondly, there will be the broken bricks, tiles, pipes and concrete. I'm only dividing these into two because, although the first category should be taken to the tip, the second can sometimes be put to very good use in a soakaway drain.

DRAINAGE

On heavy land, it may be quite clear that some provision is going to be needed to improve the drainage before you can expect to grow good crops. In the worst gardens of all, you may even need to lay a system of drains 18–24in (45–60cm) below ground. Usually, though, improving the soil structure as described in Chapter 2 is sufficient. However, that does leave us with the problem of disposing of the surface water that is draining away. In the absence of a ditch or stream at the end of the garden, the best way of coping with it

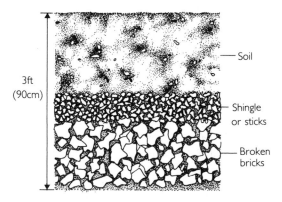

3ft (90cm)

— Soil

— Shingle or sticks

— Broken bricks

Digging a soakaway in the lowest part of the plot to help drainage.

70

is to make a soakaway in the lowest part of the plot.

A soakaway is made by digging out a pit as deep as you can manage, but certainly not less than about 3ft (1 m). It's unlikely that any of the soil from it will be worth much, because the fertile topsoil and less fertile subsoil will probably have been churned into a homogeneous mud. However, if the topsoil is still distinguishable from the sub-soil, lay it to one side on its own for return-ing last of all.

All the old bricks and things are then thrown into the hole until you've filled it to about 1 ft (30cm) from the top. If you can get some sticks or old conifer branches, these are laid on top of the bricks to stop the soil that will come next from working its way down into the soakaway. An alternative is to lift some rough or useless turf and lay this, upside-down, above the bricks; it'll have the same effect. Failing that, use a load of shingle or coarse grit.

The reason for stopping about 1 ft (30cm) below the surface is so that, obvi-ously, you won't keep plunging your spade into the soakaway and spoiling it. Then it's simply a matter of putting back sufficient soil to over-fill the hole; this will allow for natural settling. Always remember, of course, to use the topsoil you've saved in preference to subsoil. Any soil left over can be lost over the rest of the plot. And there you are, a drainage problem solved and all the rubbish gone in a single operation.

Many people ask about the best time of year for doing this heavy preliminary work. Frankly it doesn't matter; if you move in and the place is like a tip, get on with sort-ing it out. If the ground is as bad as all that, it'll become mud in the winter and con-crete in the summer anyway!

WEED REMOVAL

Once this initial clearance has been done, or if the garden didn't need it in the first place, most of the basic work is best done in the winter but, here again, don't stick to this rigidly just for the sake of it.

A plot that has already been in use but which has fallen from favour and interest can have work started on it at any time of the year because the first job is to cut it all down so that the majority of the top growth is removed. Do this with either a sickle or a scythe, and compost or burn all the rubbish so that everything is pretty well at soil level.

If this stage is reached during the grow-ing season, it is then as well to leave things for a while to allow the weeds to start growing again. This may sound mad but it is as a prelude to chemical weedkilling because the weedkiller you will be using should only be applied to actively growing weeds. If used during the winter, the weeds won't absorb it and die.

Once the regrowth is 6in or so high, therefore, treat the whole area with the weedkiller Tumbleweed or any other weedkiller based on glyphosate. This takes ten to fourteen days to show any effect, so don't expect results overnight. Once the weeds look 'sick', the ground can be dug. Alternatively you may want to leave it until the late autumn. Either way, the nature of glyphosate is such that it is inactivated by the soil, so no harmful residues are present. This means that crops can, if necessary, be sown or planted the day after treatment. Although the roots of plants treated with glyphosate will be dead, I always prefer to pick out as many of the large root systems as I can, just to be on the safe side.

The best course of action for those who would rather not use a weedkiller at this stage is probably to use a flame-thrower. This will burn off all top growth but it certainly won't kill the roots of perennial weeds. These will have to be removed carefully during digging. Although it is probably best to leave the initial digging until the autumn so that the dug surface will have the longest time to weather, this would only apply to heavy soils; you could dig light land when you like.

DIGGING

All should now be ready for digging, and this is when I make a real plea to you. Whatever the state of the garden – however long it has been empty or neglected, or even if it has been maintained in reasonable or good condition – the vegetable section at least should be double dug.

It really is very important that the soil is moved as deeply as possible and double digging is the only sensible way to do this. It doubles the depth to which roots can easily penetrate, thereby greatly improving the quality of the plants and their yield. Vegetable crops may be expected to rise by 30 per cent the season after double digging and, in the case of broad beans, they can be very nearly doubled.

Although new and neglected gardens will clearly benefit most from double digging, even established plots should be double dug every four years or so to break up the underground layer of compacted soil that develops over years of single digging.

Digging will bring some of us face to face with the first really hard piece of work and it's as well to realise that, if you're not used to it, you shouldn't go at it like a bull at a gate. This is particularly important if you aren't in the first flush of youth. The mind may be willing but that isn't a scrap of good

if the body's on its last legs. I'm perfectly serious about this; take it easy and you'll get through without any trouble. If you feel you've had enough, have a rest until you feel you are ready to start again. It doesn't matter if this isn't until the following day; if you overdo things, you'll be no good for anything and the job will never get done.

That brings us neatly on to the subject of soil cultivations. In exactly the same way that ploughing is the farmer's way of moving the soil deeply in preparation for shallower cultivations and sowing, digging is the basic soil cultivation of the gardener. It is normally carried out when the land is being worked for the first time or when a crop has just been cleared from ground already under cultivation.

A spade is the normal tool used for digging but, on heavy land, a good fork is much easier and will do the job just as well; the tool chosen for the job depends on whether or not the soil will hold together. There are several reasons for digging, the main one being to break up the soil and create a suitable tilth for sowing or planting.

Digging will also bury any weeds and weed seeds that may have grown during the life of the previous crop or before the garden came under cultivation, preventing them from germinating. It is also the most thorough and reliable way of burying bulky organic matter.

The correct way to dig is to hold the spade or fork as near vertical as is comfortable to you, so that it can be driven in to its full depth and can move the soil as deeply as this will allow. This also makes sure that anything you want to bury is nice and deep.

Digging to one spade's depth is called single digging but, in the sort of garden we looked at a little while ago, a more effective way of bringing the soil into working order

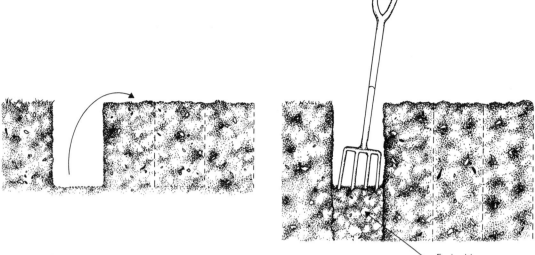

Forked layer

Single digging (left) and double digging (right). In double digging, the bottom layer is simply forked.

is by double digging. Whilst the principle for both is the same, the trench that is formed in single digging is then itself dug with a fork to a further 10–12in (25–30cm) deep.

When a reasonably large plot has to be dug, it helps to divide it in two and tackle one half at a time in the following way (see plan page 74). Dig out a trench at 'A' and pile up the soil at 'B'. The next strip of soil is turned over and forward so that it falls upside-down into trench 'A'. Continue this back along the length of the half-plot until you finish up with trench 'C'. Fill this with the soil from trench 'D' and carry on until you're left with the final trench. This is then filled with soil 'B'.

Once the land has been dug, leave it rough until shortly before you want to sow or plant. It is then broken down more finely by cultivating it with either a hand cultivator or the back of a fork. If necessary, it should be levelled in the same operation.

This will normally be all that the soil needs doing to it if you are going to be planting but, if you're going to sow, it will need raking to create a finer tilth and to remove any stones. However, don't be tempted to break it down into a finer tilth than is really needed. As a guide, where large seeds (peas and beans) are going to be sown, the ground can be left very much rougher than for small seeds (lettuces, cabbages and most other things). In fact, for peas and beans it could be left the same as for planting. This is a good habit to get into for two reasons. Firstly, it will control weed growth to some extent. If it's necessary to produce a fine tilth for the germination of small vegetable seeds, it follows that small weed seeds will need similar conditions. If, therefore, the soil surface is left rough, fewer weed seeds will germinate.

The other important reason for leaving the surface as rough as you can is that

73

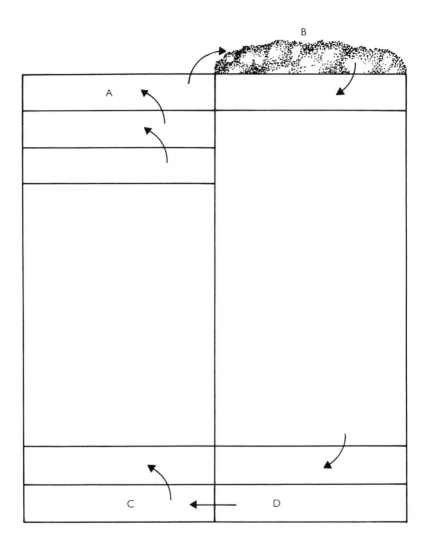

A digging plan.

clay soils in particular are less likely to 'cap'. Capping is caused by the action of heavy rain beating the surface into mud so that, when it dries out, a crust forms – clearly to the detriment of the plants. Leaving the surface rough will, to a large extent, prevent this.

Going back to digging, for a moment, you may read in old books about such things as bastard trenching and ridging. These honestly don't concern us in this day and age; they largely disappeared when estate gardens no longer had a large labour force, and in any case they were seldom, if ever, carried out in small or domestic gardens. For the most part, they were different systems used during winter digging to help the soil to be weathered by exposing a greater surface area.

Raking the soil to make a good seed bed.

Normal digging, either single or double, provides perfectly adequate weathering. It is the time left for weathering and how successfully nature carries it out that counts, not the system of digging used.

SOWING

We now come to sowing, clearly one of the most fundamental and important tasks connected with gardening and one which, interestingly enough, is often done far better by young children than by adults. The reason for this is very probably because they get on and do it rather than messing about and worrying about if they're doing it right.

The three essential things a seed needs in order to germinate are warmth, moisture and oxygen. These are provided by the sun, the rain and the air; simple but vital. When sowing, therefore, the first thing to do is to get the tilth sufficiently fine so that the seeds are, as it were, encased in soil but can still breathe. It's no use having a tiny seed sitting on top of a clod of earth; both the seed and the soil are going to dry out quickly, and that won't help germination. Next, the seed must be buried at the right depth. This is achieved, in most cases, by making a drill (groove) in the soil, sowing the seeds in the bottom and then covering them with soil.

The depth at which you should sow the seed is often given on the seed packet but, when in doubt, it's a good rule to bury the smaller seeds at a depth of roughly half an inch, certainly no deeper. At this depth they will be kept moist and reasonably warm and will have plenty of air. If they're put in any deeper, they could have a problem in fighting their way to the surface and, if sown in the spring, they might lie too wet and cold.

Although experienced and older gardeners normally use a draw-hoe to take out the actual drill beginners will probably find it simpler with a stick; it's easier to handle and you're closer to the work. In either event, always use a line to work to, making sure that it is taut and that it is the recommended distance from the row next to it.

The gap between two different types of vegetable should be midway between the two recommended planting distances. The way to work this out is to take the average of the two distances. For example, if one vegetable is in rows 1 ft (30cm) apart and the ones you're sowing need to be 2ft (60cm) apart, leave an 18in (45cm) gap between the two types. It sounds more complicated than it is.

Beans are easy enough to sow because they're grown as individual plants and are, therefore, sown individually. Peas are almost as easy because you should aim at 6–8 seeds per square foot.

Smaller seeds are a little more tricky but, whether they're being sown where the plants are to mature (*in situ*) or for transplanting later elsewhere, you should try to average about three seeds per inch (2.5cm) of drill. The art is to have the resulting seedlings well spaced but not so far apart that space is wasted.

You'll find it easiest to sow small seeds by pouring some from the packet into the palm of one hand and taking a pinch of seeds with the forefinger and thumb of the other. Rub them together and the seeds will fall. Alternatively you can sow straight from the packet, but this really hasn't got any obvious advantages – it's whatever you feel happiest doing.

With the seeds sown, soil is raked back into the drill to cover them. This is then tamped down gently with the flat of the rake to be sure the soil is in good contact with the seeds.

Watering in the seeds can be done in a number of ways but it should certainly involve the use of a watering can with a fine rose, important to avoid puddling the soil over the seeds and, perhaps, capping it.

Some people like to water the drill before sowing the seeds; others water after the seeds are sown but before they're covered in, yet others, and I'm one of them, prefer to water when the soil is firmed down and the line is out of the way. This way, you're not touching any wet soil so there's no risk of getting in a mess.

If you're sowing during March, when the weather is definitely unpredictable and often cold, it's a good idea to cover the sown rows with either cloches or polythene tunnels. These keep the ground warm and prevent rain wetting it too much. Once the seedlings are well through, take off the covering to prevent them becoming weak and drawn in growth.

SOWING IN SITU/TRANSPLANTING

Although the natural way to grow vegetables would appear to be from seeds that are sown where the plants are to mature, this can be very wasteful of space and, indeed, it can also mean later crops. Celery and early lettuces are examples of this; by sowing them in the greenhouse or indoors, and planting them out later, they mature much earlier than if sown outside.

When seeds are sown for later transplanting, you only need to sow a few at any one time; as little as 1–2ft (30–60cm) of row is often enough to provide you with sufficient plants for a whole season's needs.

Vegetables which are normally transplanted in this way include brassicas (cabbage, cauliflower, Brussels sprouts, sprouting broccoli, kale, savoy), early lettuces, celery and celeriac, leeks, tomatoes, sweet corn, marrows and cucumbers.

Vegetables which should always be grown *in situ* include beetroot, carrots, swedes, turnips, summer and autumn lettuces, parsnips, radishes, potatoes, shallots, spinach and spinach beet.

Some vegetables can be raised either way. For early cropping, they should be started in warmth and later planted out but, if time doesn't matter or if you haven't the facilities, sowing them where they are to mature is fine; it merely delays maturity. In this category we find French and runner beans, early peas, herbs, onions, sweet corn and marrows.

After outdoor sowing and watering, germination should follow in 7–14 days, according to the air and soil temperature.

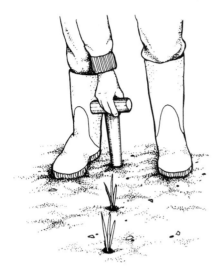

Using a dibber to plant leeks.

If the resulting seedlings are to be trans-planted, the sooner this is done (within reason), the better; small plants will establish quicker than larger ones, and with the least check to growth. If they are left too long, they'll make poor plants and some will be encouraged to bolt because of the check they receive.

As a general rule, seedlings which were raised under cover in seed trays or pots are best transplanted with a trowel. They need firm planting, but not too excessive, and little root disturbance.

On the other hand, most vegetable plants raised outside, and especially bras-sicas, must be planted firmly so that they grow 'hard', as opposed to soft and lush. Don't try to be kind and gentle to them, be really firm and always use a dibber to plant them, pushing in the soil hard round the roots. This is particularly important for Brussels sprouts. After planting out, make sure that all plants are watered well to get them off to a good start.

Those vegetables that are to grow to maturity where they're sown will also need attention, but of a different kind; they'll need thinning and singling. This is done as soon as the seedlings are large enough to handle so that those which are to remain are sub-jected to the least possible crowding.

Personally, I don't go by the book here; instead of thinning to the recommended distance in one operation, I normally thin to half that distance, wait a couple of weeks or so and then, when I know that all the plants are growing well, pull out every other one. This is a safety measure, in case any die after the first thinning. Added to that, I leave lettuces at half the distance until they're touching in the row and then use alternate plants as an early crop. The remainder are left to mature.

After planting out or thinning, it's largely plain sailing, whilst paying adequate atten tion to pest, disease and weed control, which I'll be dealing with next.

The only thing left to mention is the practice of mulching. This isn't practised very often amongst vegetables, but there are some which will appreciate it. These are mainly peas and beans, which carry on cropping for quite a considerable time. The main aim is to maintain an adequately moist root run so that the plants don't stop growing. Mulching will, of course, also keep down the weeds.

8 Pest, Disease and Weed Control

Although some people certainly worry about the use of so-called artificial fertilisers, it isn't really until we come to pest, disease and weed control chemicals that they get really worked up.

This isn't the place to become embroiled in the pros and cons of the argument for and against these materials; an awful lot has been written and spoken on the subject, and no doubt the arguments will go on. However, a look at the situation as it stands today may help gardeners to make up their own mind.

For a start, it would be as well to define what we're talking about – basically, pesticides. These are chemicals which are used, in this case, by gardeners to protect plants against attacks from pests and diseases and to kill weeds.

My own methods are perfectly simple and straightforward. I use as few pesticides as I can, in line with good gardening. That is, I adopt cultural methods of controlling the 'nasties' (pests, diseases and weeds) but, if these fail, I then call on the help of chemicals.

I am first and foremost a horticulturist and I have no intention of seeing the plants I am growing suffer. Chemicals are a perfectly legitimate aid to gardening, and a very valuable one, but their use should be as a last, rather than first, resort. I am completely opposed to their wholesale use purely as a matter of course, simply because the owner of the plants can't be bothered to use non-chemical methods of control.

The control of pests and diseases is very different to that of weeds so we will look at them separately.

PESTS AND DISEASES

The first thing that every gardener must understand and learn to live with is that pests and diseases are always with us. That is to say, no matter how tight a rein we keep on things, there are always going to be nasties about. Trying to attain one hundred per cent control of them will worry you into an early grave. A good gardener will be prepared to tolerate a certain amount of trouble but will know when and how to act. There are two approaches to the problem of pests and diseases; prevention and cure.

Prevention

Preventing pests and diseases from attacking our plants is clearly better than having to join them in battle once they are established. By that time they will have built up their strength and caused damage to a greater or lesser extent. They will be far harder to get rid of and, if chemicals are to be used, a greater quantity will be needed to overcome them.

Prevention should therefore be the watchword, and top of the list of priorities is that all plants must be grown as well as is humanly possible. A strong plant is much better able to withstand, and even in some cases repulse, attacks from its enemies.

Growing better plants will involve several things, but the most essential must be to maintain an open and fertile soil with adequate nutrient and organic matter levels. If the roots can flourish, so should the top.

Keeping plants well watered and fed is an obvious way of helping them to grow better, but it is not generally appreciated that besides the normal suffering that a lack of water inflicts, wilting plants give off a stronger scent than turgid plants (those fully charged with water). This is especially important with a vegetable like the carrot, because its main pest, the carrot fly, is attracted largely by smell. If wilting is allowed to take place during and straight after the seedlings are thinned, pests are much more likely.

Always, therefore, water plants thoroughly after thinning or moving so that they recover as quickly as possible. Not only will this mean that they receive a minimal check but also they will be less susceptible to certain scent-attracted pests.

Likewise, all root crops should be kept as evenly moist as possible throughout their growing season. Sudden soakings after long periods of drought encourages splitting. This will happen with tomatoes, also gooseberries and currants, and besides the actual splitting, the wounds will be the entry point and breeding grounds for fungus diseases such as parsnip canker.

Along with growing plants under conditions in which they will thrive, we must also do everything we can to avoid those conditions that encourage the presence, development and spread of pests and diseases.

Although this is usually more applicable to a greenhouse than to the open garden, in that adequate ventilation is the best disease preventer, it can also apply outside. Never, for example, allow seedlings to become overcrowded – it leads to them becoming drawn and weak and can frequently create a micro-climate that allows pests and diseases to flourish. Overcrowding can easily be avoided by sowing thinly and by transplanting or thinning out the seedlings as soon as is reasonably possible.

Not only will overcrowded seedlings and young plants create an environment favouring the nasties but, by being close together and touching, trouble, when it strikes, will spread like wild fire. Fungus diseases, such as Botrytis (Grey Mould), thrive in the close and cool atmosphere created by overcrowding. You only have to think of strawberries in a wet summer to appreciate that.

When hoeing amongst plants, be careful to avoid nicking them with the hoe. This not only scars root crops like turnips and beet, it also provides a perfect point of entry for fungus diseases and, frequently, for slugs.

Garden hygiene in general is extremely important. If bits and pieces of dead vegetation are allowed to lie around the garden they will quickly attract disease and can often provide top quality homes for slugs and snails. In particular, badly diseased and dead plants must be removed as soon as possible. If they are left where they are, they simply act as a source of further infection. Plants infected with serious disease should then be consigned to the dustbin or, better still, burnt.

A rather more specialised form of preventing the spread of infection concerns virus diseases. Although this is more applicable to raspberries and the like, a number of vegetables, principally lettuce, are also notorious for catching viruses. They're usually spread by infected seed but can also be carried from one plant to another by contaminated tools as well as by green-fly and other insect pests, passing on the organism by feeding on the plant's sap. Therefore, never knowingly use the same tool for dealing with healthy plants after handling infected ones.

Tobacco Mosaic virus of tomatoes is a very common example of this mistake. Cutting off side shoots from an infected plant and then using the same knife straight afterwards on a healthy plant is asking for trouble. Pruning tools, such as saws and secateurs, can also carry viruses from infected to previously healthy stock.

Something often ignored by garden-ers is the fact that most pests and diseases attack more than one crop. Putting it a bit more technically, they have alternative hosts. Clearly, there is very little to be gained in protecting a crop from this or that pest or disease if another plant is the source of infection.

These other hosts are normally other plants in the vicinity of the crop but they could equally well be over the fence in the next door garden. This is a distinct possibil-ity that should not be ignored.

Normally, however, it is just a question of, for example, club root disease of brassicas also being perfectly happy on the roots of ornamentals, like wallflowers, or weeds like shepherd's purse. Nor is it only diseases; cer-tain pests are also guilty of maintaining more than one home. Most greenfly are just as happy eating weeds as they are lettuces, for instance. Never ignore or treat this aspect of pest and disease control lightly; it is just as important as any other.

We now come to crop rotation, the prac-tice of not growing the same crop, or even type of crop, on the same bit of land every year, as a means of reducing the number of unwelcome invaders. In the present context it is a way of preventing a build up of specific diseases. These are not diseases like the mil-dews that attack the tops of plants but are essentially soil-borne ones like white rot of onions and club root of brassicas, which go for the underground parts.

If susceptible crops are grown on the same land the year after an attack, there are no prizes for guessing that the disease will turn up again, and worse. Nor is it the least bit of good practising crop rotation if alternative hosts are allowed to survive to carry over an infection to the next year.

There is also a less obvious side to rotation. Some of the soil-borne diseases have only a limited life in the soil in the absence of a suitable host. Unfortunately, though, club root is not one of them.

It used to be thought that the number of soil pests was also reduced by crop rotation. Whilst this might happen to a small extent with largely immobile creatures like wire-worm, the vast majority are active enough to move on and find another home when the need arises. In many cases this will be the same kind of vegetable which is now growing in a different part of the plot.

The last method of what we call 'cul-tural' pest and disease control concerns the varieties of vegetables that we grow. Despite what cynics might think and say, modern plant breeders are putting all their resources into the creation of vari-eties that are either resistant or immune to attack from as many pests and diseases as is humanly possible. Clearly other con-siderations have to be borne in mind as well but that feature is very high on the list of priorities. This is achieved to a large extent by delving back into the mists of time and finding any wild species of plants that exhibit a tendency to throw off attacks by nasties.

One of the most exciting discoveries some years ago was in Central Europe where a wild brassica was found to be resistant to club root. This has given rise to a number of new and resistant cultivated brassicas, the first of which was the kale 'Trixie'. Undoubtedly there will be more and better varieties.

Most gardeners also know about dis-ease-resistant varieties of tomato. These have all but done away with many of the more serious soil borne diseases as well as disorders like greenback, blotchy ripening, and bronzing. Another example is parsnip canker and the parsnip varieties 'Avon-resister' and 'Gladiator' both show good resistance to it. Fruit crops are also coming into this picture a lot more now.

Wherever possible, therefore, always use varieties that are resistant or even immune to the worst pests and diseases. There are extremely few varieties of vegetable which are actually immune to a disease, but some vegetables are definitely more resistant.

Cure

At the present time, no matter how many precautions you take or how seriously you take them, it is inevitable that every garden will get its fair share of pests and diseases. The problem then arises as to what should be done to combat them.

Even without using chemicals, there are several things that we can do but, above all, we must do them quickly. The top priority, therefore, is to keep a sharp eye open for any trouble and to act the moment you see it. The idea that you'll wait until you can be bothered or can find the time is useless; every hour that action is put off will allow whatever it is to get worse. In the case of a fungus dis-ease, this means it spreading further on the original victim and probably getting on to

other plants. With pests, a delay in action will mean this as well but it is also possible that breeding or egg laying will take place.

Always remember that the more deep seated a problem becomes, the harder it is to control. The simple and obvious thing to do when a disease is seen is to pick off and burn the infected leaf, flower, fruit or what-ever it is. This will prevent it spreading.

If the disease is really well established and has infected the stem of the plant, the only sensible course is to pull the thing up and destroy it. It may seem unnecessarily harsh but, if left, it is simply going to make matters worse by spreading to others, with-out any hope of saving the original plant.

PESTS

Non-Chemical Control

Much the same goes for the control of pests; the radical course of action is often the best – if you can pick off the offender, do so and tread on it. If you're squeamish then you have to close your eyes and squash it where it is. There is no point in being faint-hearted about it; use your fingers or, if you cannot stand that, put on some gloves. Whatever 'method' you adopt, the result is the same – a dead pest that will cause you no more bother.

This essentially physical approach to the problem of pest control is not to everyone's liking but there is no denying that two half-bricks administer a considerably quicker, more humane and more definite end to slugs than does a sprinkling of salt. However, slug traps consisting of sunken jam jars half filled with beer are a good compromise. They're effective, clean and non-chemical.

Caterpillars, too, are very quickly disposed of by picking them off the plants individually and destroying them as you

Cardboard brassica collars will prevent the cabbage root fly laying its eggs.

think best. Treading on them is definitely terminal and not too distasteful.

Another non-chemical control concerns the cabbage root fly. This is the pest that lays its eggs at soil level, these hatch out and the young grubs eat away the roots, causing the collapse and death of the plant. Soil insecticides are available for this but a non-chemical control is to place collars round the neck of transplanted brassicas. These can be bought or made from old felt, about 4in (10cm) across. Cut a slit to the centre of the disc and slip it round the neck of the transplanted plant. The fly can't now lay its eggs against the stem so it goes elsewhere.

Old Wives' Tales and Natural Controls

Amongst what might be termed 'alternative' methods of combating this, that and the other nasty, come the old wives' tales. They shouldn't be taken too seriously, but nor must they be totally ignored because, if all else fails, they could well work and solve the problem.

Many books have been written about these sometimes rather bizarre methods of preventing or banishing problems and they are certainly worth reading. It does not always do to take them too seriously, though, as some are very definitely written tongue-in-cheek. On the other hand, they must all be based on fact or they would not have survived so long and held such wide acceptance.

Here are a few to get you thinking. 'To keep club root disease away from brassicas, bury a stick of rhubarb near the crop.' I cannot follow this one at all. Club root is a disease that is encouraged by acidic soil conditions and anything more acidic than rhubarb is hard to imagine. The best control of club root is certainly to reduce the acidity of the soil by regular applications of chalk or lime.

'To get rid of peach leaf curl, pick off the infected leaves and hang mothballs or naphthalene anti-moth rings in the trees.' Never tried this myself, but it seems odd that an insecticide should also be effective against a fungus disease. Still, this is not unheard of and a coal-tar derivative (naphthalene) would certainly have the properties of a steriliser.

There are many more reputed remedies for pests than there are for diseases, one of the best known being garlic against greenfly. The normal recommendation is to plant a garlic clove amongst the plants you want to protect. Something within the garlic is exuded into the soil and then absorbed by the roots in much the same way as is a systemic insecticide. Apparently, garlic only smells when in flower so, provided that you take the precaution of removing the flower heads as soon as they appear, there should be no bother.

Personally, I cannot stand garlic at any price, and given the choice would settle for the greenfly and set about their destruction by some more orthodox means. Other members of the onion family are said to be effective, but not to the same extent. Chives would probably look the least out of place of any.

Another quite well-known remedy is French marigolds (or any other Tagetes) in the greenhouse to keep whitefly away from tomatoes and fuchsias. A lot of people still swear by this, so it is well worth a try. Another possible cure for the same problem is nasturtium plants.

Nasturtiums are also allegedly a good cure for woolly aphis in apple trees. I find this particularly hard to swallow as nasturtiums frequently get plastered with black-fly themselves, and woolly aphid is simply another variety of the same pest.

If you believe the next one, you will believe anything. 'Caterpillars originate in Tartary to the east of the Caspian Sea and are carried here on the east wind. Wind-breaks erected to keep this wind at bay will protect a garden from caterpillars.' There just isn't an answer to that.

Possibly the most widely followed remedies are the plant associations such as garlic amongst the roses. There are several of these and their devotees have almost maniacal faith in them. It would be quite wrong to write them off as useless but I have never heard of a single one that has worked for everybody and they must certainly be brought into operation before there is any sign of the problem. In other words, they may help to ward off an attack of a particular pest or disease but they will not get rid of one after it has struck.

Probably the most sensible explanation of all as regards these somewhat off-beat remedies is not that the pests are discouraged in some way but that their natural enemies are drawn into the area by the scent. This is much more feasible and would go a long way towards explaining why they sometimes work and sometimes don't – when they don't, it

could simply be because there just aren't any 'goodies' near enough to be attracted.

Although the more zealous and imaginative might flatter this whole plant association system with the title of biological control, a far more effective, and widely practised, method is to use the natural enemies of the pest, in a rather different way to that in which plant association might work. This has been done commercially for some years in glasshouses but the big snag is that this is the only place where it can be carried out with any chance of success.

The reason for this is obvious; you would have no control over the 'goodies' in the open air and most would simply disappear. Two that have been used widely under glass, both of which are available to amateurs, are the natural predator of the glasshouse red spider mite (Phytoseiulus) and a parasite of the glasshouse whitefly (Encarsia). Both are very effective at their job but the system as a whole has certain drawbacks, the main one being that it is difficult to control other pests by any chemical means without upsetting the goodies.

In the open garden, the nearest we can really get to this Utopian arrangement in which good always prevails over evil is to encourage the naturally occurring predators and parasites. Unfortunately, this has to be done in a rather negative way because the only method of attracting, for example, ladybirds, is to keep a thriving aphis population. Rather self-defeating. Really, the only thing we can do to encourage natural pest control is to avoid using sprays that will kill the predators and parasites.

Spraying

As a rule, the best type of chemical to use on vegetables is one that you first dilute and then apply with a sprayer. If only a small

PEST	HOST PLANT
aphids (greenfly, blackfly)	most crops
cabbage root fly	brassicas
carrot fly	carrots and parsnips
caterpillars	mainly brassicas
cut worms	many plants at soil level
flea beetle	seedlings; mainly brassica
millepedes	pea and bean seeds
pea moth	peas
slugs and snails	many crops
whitefly	tomatoes
wireworms	potatoes and other root vegetables

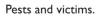

Pests and victims.

FUNGUS	HOST PLANT
botrytis (grey mould)	mainly lettuces
canker	parsnips
club root	brassicas
damping off	many seedlings
potato blight	potatoes and tomatoes
tomato leaf mould	tomatoes
white rot	onions and leeks

Fungal diseases and victims.

A sprayer is the most effective and economical way of treating rows of vegetables.

quantity of spray is needed, choose a product that can be mixed in small quantities. If, perhaps, you only need enough to treat a couple of growing-bags, even small quantities of diluted chemicals could be too much so it's probably wiser to buy either an appropriate aerosol or a material already diluted and sold in a hand sprayer. Some people think this approach is much too expensive. It is only expensive if you have need of a lot more chemical. In that case, it's obviously cheaper to mix up some of your own. For treating the odd few plants, though, the aerosol is made for the job and anything else is probably very wasteful.

If all other things are satisfactory and appropriate, use a systemic insecticide or fungicide rather than a contact one. The contact kind will only kill pests or fungi with

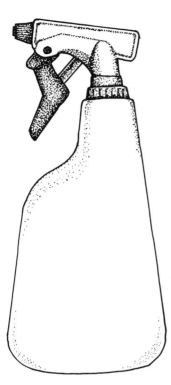

Hand sprayers containing ready-diluted insecticides are first rate for treating minor outbreaks.

which it comes in contact; a systemic is absorbed by the plant and passed round in the sap stream to reach unsprayed places.

Whatever you do, though, *always* read and understand the label before you buy the material and again before you use it. It only takes a minute and you can then be sure that you are using the right one.

Although most materials are sold as sprays, you may also find some as dusts. These are all right where only small quantities are wanted (as with aerosols) but the snag about them is that they leave a far from pretty deposit on the plants. If you don't mind this, they're fine. The other type you'll see are smokes, these are for use solely in greenhouses. Not only could they be harmful outside, they're also useless.

When it comes to choosing a product, it is best to ask the advice of your garden centre as this area is constantly changing and developing.

There are important rules to observe when spraying.

1 Avoid spraying during bright sunshine as this can cause scorch to the plants' leaves. Even plain water can do this, as it is caused simply by the magnification of the sun through the water or spray droplets.
2 Don't spray on a windy day; the spray will very likely be carried on to another crop for which it may not be appropriate.
3 Don't spray peas, beans, marrows, or any other vegetable that may be in flower, until the evening and make sure then that bees have finished working the flowers for the night.
4 Many sprays will kill beneficial and harmless insects as well as pests. Learn to recognise a few of the most common and try to avoid spraying when they're present. These include ladybirds, lacewings, hover-flies, centipedes, most large beetles and the devil's coach-horse (rove beetle).
5 When you spray, make sure that the whole plant is thoroughly covered, even with systemic sprays. It's always best to get good coverage rather than rely on the characteristics of the material. The systemic action should be regarded as a bonus rather than be taken as a matter of course.
6 Don't spray when the plants are wet from rain or when rain is expected the same day.
7 When using an aerosol, *don't* try to wet the foliage as this will usually result in scorching the plant. Just drift the spray through the leaves in the same way that you would use a fly aerosol indoors.

Those are the main points to observe when spraying, but undoubtedly the most important of all is to use common sense and to pay attention to what you are doing. That way, accidents and mishaps are avoided.

Storage

The safe keeping of garden chemicals is just as important as is their use. Here again, though, common sense is really the key.

1   Keep them well out of reach of children and pets.
2   Don't store any near food.
3   Never keep, or even allow, weedkillers in a greenhouse. Accidental spillages can occur and even the fumes of some can cause damage to plants.
4   Always keep them in the original containers.
5   Read the instructions before use and obey them, particularly with regard to safety.
6   Avoid keeping the containers where they can get very hot, such as in direct sunshine.
7   Store the containers in a frost-free place during the winter.
8   Never use chemicals that are intended for farmers and commercial growers. Some gardeners think it's clever and that it saves money getting a bottle of, say, weedkiller from a farmer or grower friend. Apart from being extremely dangerous and stupid, *it is against the law and prosecutions can follow.*

WEED CONTROL

Weed control is just as important as controlling other enemies of plants that try to gain the upper hand. We've already seen that weeds can provide alternative homes for a whole army of pests and diseases but they'll do a great many other unpleasant things besides that.

They are strong competitors for the water and plant foods which are needed by the vegetables we're growing. If the weeds are using the same raw materials, that means less for our crops. Then there's the direct effect that weeds have on the growth of the vegetables. If weeds are allowed to grow too large, they will draw up the vegetables so that they become weak and spindly. If they're growing amongst young plants, they can even smother them.

If, perish the thought, the weeds are allowed to flower and set seed, they're likely to spread further afield and into other areas of the garden. On top of all that, they look slovenly and give a general air of dereliction to the garden.

Fortunately, weed control is a pretty easy and straightforward operation but it can still be divided into two main methods – mechanical and chemical.

The cheapest and most effective method of weed control.

Most of us rely on hoes, definitely a mechanical means of control, to keep the weeds down but even with this there's a right way and a wrong way of going about it. Hoeing should be done the moment weed seedlings are visible. In this way they are very easily killed and so are thousands more that you can't even see.

Always hoe before the weeds are in flower but if, for any reason, they are large and nearly flowering, they should be hoed and then raked off and composted before they do actually flower. Semi-mature weeds left lying on the ground can remain alive and flower if the weather is damp.

Never hoe deeply; the object of the operation is to sever the weed from its roots just below the surface. That is the surest way of killing them. Only hoe when the soil is dry; wet soil will simply clog up the hoe and the weeds will never be killed; they will simply be transplanted.

Always hoe carefully so that wanted plants are not damaged. Keep all hoes sharp; they are cutting tools and, as such, are useless when blunt.

Another non-chemical system that most certainly should not be ignored is the use of mulches. Mulching not only saves the time taken up with hoeing but it also enables weed control to go on at a time when hoeing would be impossible, in other words when the soil is wet. In addition, it will help the soil to retain moisture and stop it capping.

If a bulky organic mulch is used, it has the added benefit of improving the soil. Garden compost is the most popular material and this has already been fully dealt with. Well-rotted manure is also excellent but 'well rotted' is the key phrase to all organic mulches. Putting down a mulch of only semi-rotted material isn't a good idea at all. For a start, it looks untidy but, far worse than that, it could well carry live weed seeds, leading to a considerably worse mess than before.

It is not really feasible, or even sensible, to put a mulch of this sort down amongst every type of vegetable. Those most likely to benefit are longstanding crops like peas, beans and brassicas, and even sweet corn. These are all reasonably tall vegetables and a mulch will fit beneath them quite easily and do a lot of good. Aim to make the mulch 3–4in (8–10cm) deep.

A complete departure from organic matter involves the use of black polythene. It can be used between more or less any vegetable and has all the benefits of an organic mulch except that it doesn't supply organic matter.

One of its best and most labour-saving uses is covering potatoes in place of earthing them up. The polythene is laid down in the spring along the rows that the spuds are going to occupy and the 'seed' potatoes are planted through slits that you make in the polythene. The darkness stops the tubers going green and all you have to do is keep an eye on their progress by lifting the polythene occasionally.

When used between vegetables, polythene should be punctured with a fork so that rain is able to pass through it. If this is not done, the soil would become dry and you would find puddles lying about all over the surface. Potatoes will be all right because they have the slits through which they're planted but make sure that the water runs through and doesn't lie in puddles. You can in fact buy ready-perforated black polythene. By the way, don't use clear polythene for a mulch; this will simply behave like a greenhouse and encourage the weeds to grow.

Moving on to chemical weedkillers – there are, in fact, mercifully few which are recommended for use amongst edible crops. Among those that are, I would single out Scotts 'Weedol' and glyphosate as being outstanding. Weedol is used to kill annual and seedling perennial weeds; glyphosate is the answer to established perennials, though it will also kill the others. Both are inactivated by the soil so leave no residues harmful to plants. This means that they can be used quite safely amongst standing crops, provided that they are not allowed to come into contact with the actual crop plants.

These two weed killers can also be used on ground that is earmarked for sowing or planting as this can take place the day after treatment. The main differences between them are that Weedol acts within hours and is more of a 'contact' material by killing only the above-ground parts of the plant that it lands on. Glyphosate, as we've already seen, takes a week or so to work and is systemic, in that it moves around within the weed and kills the roots as well.

Apart from the initial ground clearance, the uses for glyphosate amongst vegetables are rather limited. Perennial weeds like docks and thistles are much better dug up by hand. However, bindweed and ground elder, especially in a wet summer, are difficult to hoe to death whereas glyphosate will get rid of them without any bother. Weedol is ideal for killing small weeds that are growing between rows of vegetables when the ground is too wet for hoeing.

Neither of these, nor any other weedkiller, should be regarded as a substitute for hoeing; they are merely methods of weed control that can be adopted when hoeing, for one reason or another, can't be carried out.

The same policy should be adopted with weedkillers as with insecticides and fungicides; they should only be used when other methods fail and they should be used with great care.

Applying Weedol with a dribble bar to kill weeds between rows of vegetables where hoeing is impossible or inadvisable.

9 Different Ways of Growing Vegetables

This chapter encompasses all the different growing systems that you as a gardener are likely to come across and use.

CLOCHES AND TUNNELS

These are very cheap and simple aids for protecting vegetables which are either already established and growing or which have just been put in. They can even be used where no crop yet exists.

In the past, most cloches were made of glass with thick wires holding them together. They were rather like Chinese puzzles to put together and it was quite a hazardous job, even for the experienced gardener. Now, plastic has more or less replaced glass; and a good thing too! It's lighter and far stronger and, even if it costs more than glass to buy, it hardly ever needs replacing. It's much safer too.

The type of tunnels to use are the ones where polythene sheeting is stretched over

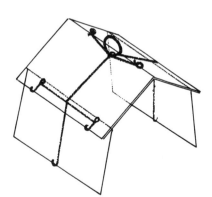
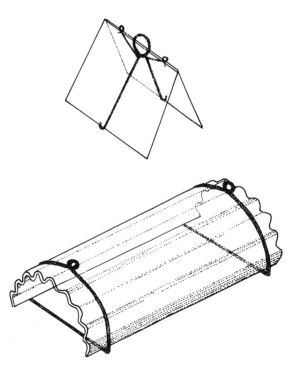

Glass and plastic cloches.

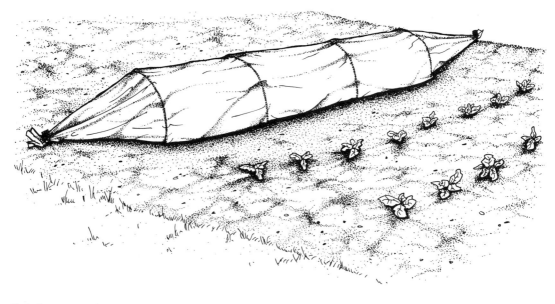

Polythene tunnel.

wire hoops. The original ICI polythene tunnels are no longer sold but many modern variations are available and any large garden centre will be able to help you. I still have some of the original hoops and use new polythene over them. Cloches and tunnels can be useful all the year round, but the spring is the most logical time to start.

The main problem is getting the soil into a warm and workable condition so that seeds may be sown and plants put in when they should be. One would normally regard March as being the start of the gardening season for the year. In February, therefore, which is often a dryish month, keep your eyes open and, when you see that the soil is drying out, cover the width of a few rows with cloches or tunnels so that the ground is kept dry and warms up in readiness for sowing in mid-March. This will enable you to make the best use of the ground so that the vegetables can go in when they're due to, rather than when

the ground is ready for them, which could be in late April.

Once the seeds and/or plants are in, you can choose for yourself whether or not you want to replace the covering, but personally I like to keep them protected until either the seeds are up or the plants are well established and growing away. This is normally a fortnight or so after sowing or planting. It isn't a good idea to keep plants covered beyond that point or they could become weak and drawn. All we're doing is protecting them from the worst of the weather so that they grow well and mature on time. Besides that, if we take the cloches off then, we can use them to protect another crop.

There is, of course, the other use to which cloches can be put in the spring and that is for advancing maturity. We have to be careful over the crops we do this with but it's a very useful system for quick-growing salads like lettuces and radishes. These can remain covered for most of their life but, here again, it's best to uncover them as they approach maturity or they'll all come quickly and at once.

Don't allow it to get too hot inside the cloches or tunnels or the plants will undoubtedly suffer. Give them plenty of fresh air on sunny days but always close them up well before nightfall so that they stay warm overnight.

Larger cloches can be used to raise peas, runner or dwarf French beans and sweet corn until the plants are too big. During the summer, there'll probably be very little use for the covering so it can be cleaned and stored away until the autumn. However, larger cloches, if they are 2ft (60cm) or so wide and high, can be used for raising and maturing half-hardy crops like cucumbers, melons and marrows in the same way that you would use a cold greenhouse.

You could even extend to semi-exotics like peppers and aubergines but, whatever you decide on, do make sure that air is given whenever it's sunny or many of the plants could get scorched up and will certainly run short of water all too often.

The one thing you should never do is try to grow hardy kinds and varieties of vegetable under cover. This isn't meant to be and they'll certainly be a flop. You often see people trying to grow outdoor tomatoes under cloches and then wondering why they're all leaf and no fruit.

Managing a crop under cloches or tunnels requires more attention than does one in the open because nature isn't in charge – you are. Watering, therefore, has to be attended to regularly and, in the case of crops staying under cover, so does liquid feeding. Pest and disease control is also more exacting because they'll spread like wild-fire if allowed to develop unchecked.

Vegetables such as marrows and peppers which require to be pollinated before they'll produce any crop should be given as much air as possible once they're in flower. Not only will this keep them cool but it will also allow bees and other pollinating insects to work amongst the flowers.

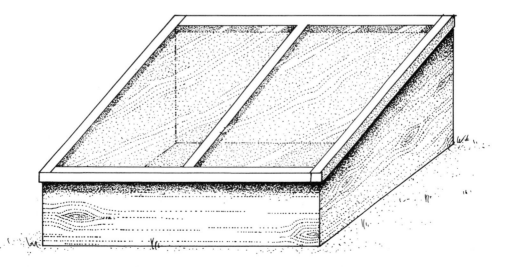

A cold frame, excellent for protecting overwintering lettuces and also for raising plants in.

Moving on in the year, we come to the autumn. This is another time when cloches and polythene tunnels can be very useful. Now, though, they are used to ensure that crops mature properly rather than for speeding up their development. Melons and such like will keep going much longer if they're covered, at least during the night when the cool September evenings arrive.

Salads can be kept going much longer under cover and outdoor tomatoes are a natural candidate for the added protection. The system to adopt with these is to wait until you see that they're taking longer to ripen. Then, spread straw on the ground under them, cut them away from their stakes and lay them down on the straw before covering them up. Once again, try initially to keep them covered only at night and when it's wet but, as it gets more into autumn, extend this as you think fit. Give them air whenever you can, though, or they'll go rotten.

During the winter, you may like to try growing lettuces under cold cover. These should be chosen carefully so that you get the right varieties, such as 'Winter Gem'. There isn't much else that can be grown under cloches during the winter so, if you're not using the cloches, clean them and put them away until the early spring.

GROWING-BAGS

Although you can adapt more or less any container to grow some sort of vegetable, the growing-bag is certainly the one that I'd recommend, especially for beginners. They have been made to a specification and are streets ahead of anything you can make up yourself.

Although growing-bags for gardeners were introduced in the mid-1970s, it's surprising how many people still have problems with them. They'll quite happily grow plants of all sorts in pots, tubs, window boxes and troughs but can't get the idea into their head that a growing bag is simply another sort of container, for which exactly the same rules and techniques apply.

What to Grow

As far as vegetables are concerned, virtually all can be grown in bags but, obviously, some are far more suitable than others. Some people think it necessary to compare the cost of the bag with the value of the crop. However, because bags sometimes represent the only way in which you can grow any vegetables in an otherwise floral garden, this isn't always as important as it might at first appear to be. Anyway, most growing-bags cost less than a pint of beer.

Clearly, one would still aim at growing the higher priced vegetables and, without a doubt, tomatoes are the most popular. Peppers and aubergines (egg plants) are also easy but don't try to grow them outdoors in the open; whatever you may hear, they just aren't a success. A cold greenhouse is probably the best place, though tall cloches can also work.

Sow peppers and aubergines as and when you would tomatoes. Prick them out straight into small (3½in/9cm) pots and then into one just over 4¼in/11 cm. Both will naturally form bushy plants but aubergines are sometimes reluctant to send out side shoots so the tops should be pinched out when they're about 6in (15cm) tall. They should be planted in the bags at the same stage as you would tomatoes, when the first flowers are open. Help pollination by tapping the stems to release the pollen – again, as you would tomatoes.

Drainage

The business of drainage probably raises more queries than anything else but really it's quite simple. There should only be a need to make arrangements for drainage if, for some reason completely unrelated to growing-bags, you simply cannot get the hang of watering and perpetually give far too much. Under these circumstances, a few slits 1in (2.5cm) long can be made in the *side* of the bag just below the overhang. Even this, though, should only be done as a last resort.

Holes made in the base of the bag lead to the need for more watering and feeding during the summer and, in the case of tomatoes, you run the risk of the roots growing out into possibly diseased soil.

Watering

The actual watering is also sometimes a sticking point with beginners; but this applies equally to pots and most other types of container. Correct watering is really the secret of success with growing-bags and it's perfectly simple. There is also plenty of latitude as to the amount of water that a bag should be given; it isn't at all critical.

The initial watering after planting should usually be about a gallon, (4½ litres). You shouldn't need to look at them for a week then, unless it's terribly hot. More detailed advice is sometimes given in the bag's instructions but, even then, the dampness of the compost will determine just how much is needed. Just try to avoid having the plants swimming.

Always avoid extremes of sopping wet and bone dry; that's bad for any plant. The real way to master the watering is to pay attention to the dampness of the compost. If about the top inch is dryish, give water; if not, don't bother.

Always water thoroughly; it should never be necessary to give less than about half a gallon (2¼ litres) and you can even wait until it will take a whole gallon. Keeping the compost evenly damp at all times is the aim, to which one must add that the plants should always have as much water as they need.

A few years ago you could buy a bag-sized plastic tray with 1–2in (2.5–5cm) high sides and ribs in the bottom. You made three slits in the bottom of the bag and wicks of capillary matting were pushed in, leaving a couple of inches hanging out. The bag was then planted up, placed on the ribs and watered. A few days later the tray was filled with water. The wicks dangled in it and were able to absorb water and pass it into the compost.

Couldn't be easier and it worked like a charm. Perhaps it was too cheap to be profitable but it was one of the finest aids to gardening in growing-bags ever devised. There should be a good market awaiting a similar product but, in the mean time, a shallow trough scraped out of the soil, lined with polythene and with three bricks placed in the bottom should work almost as well.

How Many Plants?

The number of plants per bag sometimes presents difficulties, if it isn't in the instructions. Lengthy research at Levingtons showed that the best number of tomato plants is three per bag when grown in the greenhouse and four when grown in the open. For other plants it's largely a matter of common sense but here are some examples, including a couple of fruits: runner beans, 8; cucumbers, 3; marrows and courgettes, 2; lettuces, 6–8; peppers and aubergines, 3; melons, 2–3 according to variety; strawberries, 10.

Supporting tall crops can be puzzling. However, if the bags are standing on soil, have plants toward the back of the bag and push in canes behind them outside the bag.

When on concrete at the base of a fence or wall, nails can be driven in level with the ends of the bag (or row of bags) 3–4ft (0.9–1.2m) above them. Wire is then drawn across between the nails and soft twine suspended from this above each plant and lightly tied to the stem.

There are also several proprietary devices that work very well but it is usually found that a little ingenuity is equally effective. A good system is to stand the bags on planks to the back of which are secured canes opposite each plant. This is especially handy because the bags are put on the planks at planting time and kept in the greenhouse for as long as is necessary without the risk of disturbing anything when (or if) they're moved outdoors.

Feeding

When it comes to feeding it is difficult to lay down rules because different makes of bag need different treatments. This is because the amount and type of nutrient already in the compost, its persistence and the trace element status vary.

All that can really be said about feeding is that you should use a well-known brand of liquid feed and follow the instructions on the feed container. These are sometimes at odds with those on the bags but, because feeds vary in strength, I prefer to stick to the ones on the feed rather than the sometimes rather loose ones on the bags. The simplest advice is really to buy the same make of bag and feed; that way, they're sure to agree.

Re-Using Bags

Something that is often asked about growing bags is whether they can be used for a second year? The answer has to be yes and no.

Let us say that you used the bags originally for growing tomatoes. By the end of the season, their plant food content will be completely unknown. Added to that, the compost will be run through with roots and as hard as an old mattress. Physically and chemically, therefore, the growing-bags will bear no resemblance to new ones. There's also the very real risk that there are root diseases in the compost. The prevention of soil-borne diseases was, after all, how the growing bag came about.

Put all this together and you'll see that growing long-term crops, such as tomatoes, cucumbers, melons, peppers and aubergines in 'second-hand' bags just isn't sensible. On the other hand, if the compost in the bag is chopped up and broken down, then the bag can certainly be used again for a short-term crop. This could be something like lettuces, radishes, herbs, spring flowering bulbs or even strawberries. In fact, and as a slight diversion from vegetables, strawberries do very well in a once-used growing-bag, better than in a new one, because of the abundant potash and comparative lack of nitrogen.

Bulbs such as tulips, hyacinths and daffodils can also be planted after the main crop has been pulled out in the autumn. The compost doesn't really even need to be broken up, though it does help with planting.

Conversely, a short-term crop can be grown in a new bag in the autumn/winter to be followed by the main crop in the spring or early summer. It must be said, though, that this is less satisfactory.

Wire

Three simple ways of supporting plants in growing bags.

Another frequent query concerns the uses to which the old compost can be put once a bag has been finished with. Broadly speaking, it has all the uses that peat has, except one. You can dig it into the garden, use it as a mulch, even brush it into the lawn as a top-dressing. The only thing you

shouldn't use it for is in place of new peat in home-made seed or potting compost. It isn't sterile any longer and seedlings grown in it can easily suffer.

Personally, I sieve the growing bag compost after use, store it over the winter and then rake it into the top 1–2in (2.5–5cm) of soil in the spring at sowing time. It makes all the difference to the speed and quality of germination and the seedlings are strong.

NO-DIGGING SYSTEMS

When we discussed the bed system of growing vegetables, mention was made of methods that didn't involve any digging. This might sound like the answer to many gardeners' prayers but there are snags.

For a start, the ground which is going to be used for this type of vegetable growing has to be double dug to make the drainage perfect and to get the ball rolling. The best way is to stick to the 4ft (1.2m) wide beds with 18in (45cm) paths between them, as used in the bed system. However, although the beds are lightly forked over after each crop, a 4–6in (10–5cm) layer of well-rotted garden compost is then put on them and no deep digging is done at all.

The beds rise over the years and get deeper in compost so that the quality of vegetables improves all the time. That, of course, raises another snag; you have to wait some years for the beds to get deep enough in compost and to work up a full head of steam.

The system is much favoured by 'organic' gardeners because of the amount of compost or manure that it uses but there's no reason why it shouldn't be set up in any garden, conventional or 'organic'.

The quantity of bulky organic matter required can also be a stumbling block; not everyone can make or acquire the large amounts needed. Even so, it has its attractions, the main one of course being the almost complete lack of digging once the system is working.

VEGETABLES IN THE GREENHOUSE

Growing vegetables in a greenhouse is a specialised area of gardening. The aim of this section, therefore is simply to whet your appetite and to show you what can be done with a greenhouse in the hope that you'll follow it up elsewhere.

In a rather similar way to using cloches and tunnels, greenhouses make it possible to start growing plants earlier in the year, to continue growing the less hardy ones later into the autumn and, indeed, to grow some that would otherwise be impossible.

The overwhelming uses to which amateurs' greenhouses are put are for raising and growing on plants which are to be planted out later on and for growing tomatoes. I would think this covers about half the greenhouses in the country. Oh yes, and also for housing rabbits or guinea pigs during the winter. These are obviously important and popular uses but they're also unimaginative and only take advantage of about a quarter of the potential benefits of a greenhouse.

We do, of course, have to distinguish between the heated and unheated greenhouse because, obviously, this is going to have an enormous influence on what can be grown. Broadly speaking, an unheated greenhouse is one step up from a cloche; its size is the only real difference and it can't honestly be used for anything even bordering on tricky.

Without any heat at all, seed sowing shouldn't begin before March. Not only will many seeds probably fail to germinate, the resulting seedlings will have difficulty in surviving.

As far as plant raising is concerned, a cold greenhouse of this sort should be used mainly for raising plants that are to go outside in late May after the risk of frosts is past. Good examples of these include early summer cabbage and cauliflower, celery, leeks, onions from seed, lettuces, outdoor tomatoes and cucumbers, marrows, sweet corn, dwarf French and runner beans.

More or less any brassicas can be raised in a greenhouse, and this is very useful if the soil outdoors is too wet or lumpy for sowing in, but you must remember to move the pots of seedlings outside as soon as they're up to stop them getting drawn and weak. This is especially important in the summer.

Besides their use for raising plants, unheated greenhouses are grand for growing crops of indoor tomatoes, cucumbers, melons, peppers, aubergines and winter lettuces.

It usually pays to buy these plants from a good nursery during April rather than trying to struggle to raise them yourself and ending up with a poor lot a month later than you want them. The only winter crop amongst these are the lettuces but chicory, endive and seakale can all be forced, either under the staging or some other cover in the winter along with rhubarb.

All the tomatoes and things can be grown in ordinary greenhouse border soil improved with once-used peat (such as ex-potting or ex-growing-bag compost) and grit, but results will be infinitely better if you use new growing-bags. The idea that you're somehow saving money by not using bags is a complete fallacy, as well as being a waste of time, when you look at the difference in crop weights.

If you can arrange for a little heat to be available in the greenhouse, so that it can be kept frost-free during the early spring, you'll be able to start things off earlier in the year. You can also raise your own greenhouse tomatoes. You won't find much difference in the *range* of vegetables which you'll be able

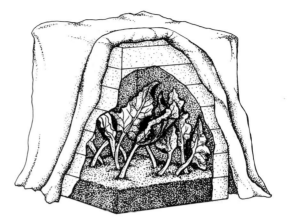

Rhubarb is an easy crop to force in a slightly heated greenhouse.

to grow but it will greatly extend the range of ornamentals.

One of the most useful pieces of equipment, especially for the beginner, is an electric propagator. This allows you to raise seedlings early in the year without having to heat the whole structure. There is then, though, the problem of keeping the seedlings alive and well once they're out of the propagator! If you want to take things even further, it's quite possible to raise and grow early crops of outdoor vegetables, such as French beans and potatoes, in the greenhouse but this demands considerable skill as both heat and the light intensity have to be taken into account.

10 Harvesting and Storage

In spite of what you may be thinking after reading all that has gone before, growing vegetables is really quite easy. It's just that there's rather a lot to think about before you get on with the actual growing.

What a shame it would be if, after all the thought and work, the finished product was spoiled, or even wasted, through a lack of knowledge as to the best way to harvest and store it. Fortunately, it won't take long to ensure against that but the points that we will be looking at are all important and are worth following if you are to get the best from your vegetable patch.

HARVESTING

A common fault, especially amongst newcomers to gardening or with established gardeners who have got into bad habits, is to leave vegetables until they are well past their best. This is the result of a natural tendency to leave them until they're 'nice and big'. This is perfectly all right with a few vegetables, such as maincrop potatoes, but it's a mistake with the majority.

What happens when most vegetables get large is that they get 'nasty and big', and coarse. Their flavour gets rank and strong and, in some cases, they can even be unpleasant to eat. Carrots, turnips and most other root vegetables become woody and fibrous and are then better suited to carpentry than to cookery.

When peas, broad beans and sweet corn get old, they lose their delicious, juicy flavour and get hard and mealy. French and runner beans become stringy and develop internal husks. The flavour of lettuces and most greens becomes strong and, very often, the plants bolt and cannot be eaten at all. A complete waste. Marrows and cucumbers get dry, fibrous and chewy.

Onions and shallots are the 'odd men out' in that, once they reach their full size, they stop growing, the foliage dies off and the bulb becomes dormant.

Therefore, with very few exceptions, always gather vegetables when they are still young and tender. You won't be losing anything, whereas you'll most certainly be losing quality if they're left purely for the sake of gaining a bit more in bulk. If they are left after they are at their best, they can only deteriorate.

By the same token, picking pre-ripe vegetables is equally wasteful. Allow things to reach their optimum size before gathering them. Another important point is that many vegetables must be picked over regularly if they are to yield their maximum crop. Peas, all beans, Brussels sprouts, sprouting broccoli, tomatoes, marrows and cucumbers are the main ones in this group. If you can't keep up with eating them, they'll still have to be picked but should then be either frozen, if appropriate, or given to friends.

Excess vegetables and allowing them to spoil with age is a particularly thorny problem when holidays are due. On no account should you go away for more than about a week without making arrangements for vegetables to be gathered when they are ready. All will be wasted and some will stop cropping.

Before you go away, though, make sure that you have picked everything that needs to be; pick harder than you would normally – there's no point in giving away more than you have to!

STORAGE

This is one of the most valuable subjects about which to have a working knowledge. Not only does successful storage prevent the waste of vegetables which all mature within a short time, it also means that you seldom have to be without at least some sort of vegetable.

If we exclude possibly the best method of storage, freezing, there really aren't many vegetables that can be kept for any length of time. The Dutch white cabbages can be

hung up in a shed, but personally I prefer to grow other varieties to give a succession of fresh cut cabbages rather than have a whole block of the Dutch for storing.

Besides this, root crops including potatoes, and onions and shallots are the only ones which store reliably. Potatoes are the easiest. Any remaining in the ground in mid-October should be lifted, dried off and stored in bags in a dry and frost-free shed or garage. If there isn't room for this, they can be what is called 'clamped' in the open.

You don't see much clamping nowadays, but it is an excellent way to store potatoes. A good layer of straw is laid on the ground, the potatoes are piled high on this and are then covered with more straw so that you end up with something looking like a small haystack. Soil is then put on the straw to hold it down and provide yet more insulation. This is beaten down with the back of a spade and all is cosy for the winter. When removing a few potatoes from the clamp to use, be sure to seal up the hole afterwards.

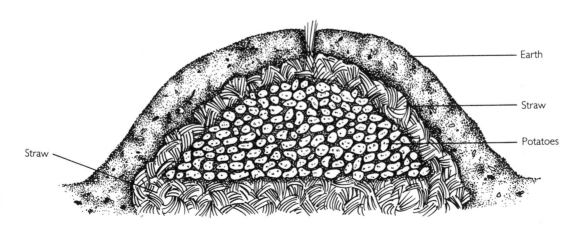

Earth

Straw

Potatoes

Straw

Clamping potatoes. Still a good way of storing large quantities.
Also suitable for other root crops.

An attractive way of storing onions.

Carrots, turnips, swedes, beetroot and parsnips can also be clamped but I prefer to leave parsnips in the ground until they're needed. You do run the risk of them being frozen into the earth during really hard spells but this can be overcome by putting straw over the rows in December and some sticks on top to stop it blowing away.

All those root crops can also be stored dry in bags as for potatoes.

Marrows can also be hung up alongside the Dutch white cabbages but, here again, I prefer to eat them fresh and turn any surplus into marrow and ginger jam.

Onions and shallots must always be well dried and ripened, if necessary in a greenhouse, and then stored in net bags or in strings. Strings are very picturesque and are quite easy to tie, but are a slight waste of time because onions should always be stored as cold as possible, frost-free, and not in a warm kitchen where they'll dry out.

11 Vegetable by Vegetable

The theoretical side of planning in the vegetable garden has already been dealt with elsewhere – but one of the first things that we have to decide is the kinds of vegetable that we would like to grow.

This is bound to be a personal choice as no two people have exactly the same likes and dislikes. However, whilst the following list is by no means complete, it does include all the most popular vegetables and those that are unlikely to go out of fashion.

You will notice that only a few of the best varieties have been named. This is deliberate, as the different seed houses have their own favourites and any selection will probably be out of date by the time you read it.

One of the most important aspects of each kind of vegetable is the recommended spacing. In many cases, these will be at variance with the instructions on the packet. Which you follow is up to you, but the ones that are given here are those recommended by the former National Vegetable Research Station, now the Institute of Horticultural Research, Wellesbourne, where for many years they carried out detailed trials to determine the optimum number of plants per square yard to give the heaviest yield of highest quality vegetables.

Very often the spacing is closer than one sees elsewhere, but the original spacing was often designed to give the best individual plants rather than combining this with the maximum yield from a given area.

My own feeling is that, for domestic use, the Wellesbourne figures are the ones to follow whereas, for the show bench, the older and wider spacing could be more appropriate.

I only mention the principal pests and diseases in this chapter.

The yields I mention are very approximate and are simply an indication of what you might expect. The yield will depend, to a certain degree, on the variety, but the deciding factor will be the way that the crop is grown.

The varieties that I am giving you in this chapter are my recommendations at the time of writing (2009). They are constantly changing as plant breeders produce new and, sometimes, better ones. Don't blame me, therefore, if they are already out of date by the time you read this!

ASPARAGUS

Asparagus is usually thought of as a luxury vegetable, but really the only thing luxurious about it is the flavour. However, a bed does take up rather a lot of room if it is to give a usable amount at one cutting.

Soil requirements Light soil is preferred but heavy land can be made quite suitable with the addition of plenty of bulky organic matter during the preparations.

Possible yield   The yield of a bed depends very much on its age. A reasonable yield in the early years would be 4–5lb (1.8–2.3kg) per 10ft (3m) of bed.

Time from planting to harvest   If planting one-year-old plants, start cutting in the third or fourth season after planting.

Varieties   'Connover's Colossal'. New Continental varieties are appearing frequently and are worth trying in milder districts.

Sowing   Although there's nothing to stop you raising plants from seed, it's much more satisfactory to buy plants from a specialist supplier.

Planting   Try to buy one-year-old plants and plant them in March or April, preferably April. There are several planting schemes; probably the easiest to follow is to plant in double rows with 18in (45cm) between plants and 18in (45cm) between rows. Plant with the crowns 6in (15cm) below the surface but cover with only 3–4in (7.5–10cm) of soil to leave the plants in a shallow dip. Never allow the roots of newly-arrived plants to dry out. Keep a damp sack etc. over them while planting.

Cultivations   Unless the beds are particularly long, hand weeding is the best system. However, mulching the beds with 3–4in (7.5–10cm) of well rotted compost each early winter will also keep the weeds to a minimum. This should be done soon after the tops have been cut down following yellowing.

Pests and diseases   Asparagus beetle larvae may eat the foliage; treat with bifenthrin. Cutworms and slugs may also be troublesome.

Harvesting   Use a saw-edged bread knife or asparagus knife to cut the shoots to about 2in (5cm) below the surface when the shoots reach about 6in (15cm) tall above the surface. Carry on cutting for 6–8 weeks depending on the age and strength of the   bed; end of June at the latest. Asparagus freezes well.

BEANS

Broad Beans

A popular and heavy-yielding crop. Given good soil conditions, they are very easy to grow well. Varieties suitable for autumn sowing are extremely hardy. They freeze excellently.

Soil requirements   Nothing in particular but good drainage and deep cultivation encourage strong root and pod development.

Possible yield   About 5½lb (2.5kg) per 10ft (3m) of row for traditional varieties. About 4.5lb (2kg) for dwarf varieties.

Time from sowing to harvest   9–11 weeks for spring sown; about 6 months for autumn sown. An autumn sowing will be ready for picking about two weeks ahead of a spring sowing.

Varieties   For spring sowing: 'Jubilee Hysor' (Windsor type) for normal (3ft. + /90cm) height, best type for flavour; 'Feligreen' – seldom more than about 2ft (60cm) tall, excellent for freezing; the 'Sutton' (Dwarf). For autumn sowing: 'Aquadulce Claudia'.

Sowing   In November or March to May. Sow tall varieties 4½in (11.5cm) apart, 2in (5cm) deep, 18in (45cm) between rows. Sow shorter varieties 9in (23cm) apart, 2in (5cm) deep, 9in (23cm) between rows. May also be sown January–March under cloches.

Transplanting   Those sown early under cover in pots or boxes can, if you like, be transplanted in April. Otherwise, sow *in situ*.

Cultivations Keep weeds down by hoeing. Never allow the plants to run short of water, particularly when the pods are forming. Provide support when the tall varieties are about 2ft (60cm) tall. This is best done with a stout cane at each corner of the bean plot, running a string round all four canes.

Overwintering varieties will greatly appreciate a cloche or polythene tunnel during the worst of the winter. Pinching the tops out of the plants when the bottom flowers have 'set' will encourage bigger and better pods and, at the same time, discourage blackfly.

Pests and Diseases The pea and bean weevil may take little bites out of the edges of the leaves; don't worry. Blackfly is the worst pest. Chocolate spot fungus may appear late in the season, seldom in large enough quantities to warrant control measures.

Harvesting Never allow the beans to become coarse and mealy, always pick them young and tender. Old age is shown by the development of a black scar on the seed and the toughening and discolouring of the pod. Broad beans freeze very well so there's no excuse for letting them get old and tasteless.

French Beans

A very popular summer vegetable that starts after broad beans but before runner beans. Like runner beans, the whole pod is eaten.

Soil requirements No particular soil needs, but it shouldn't be too firm or the roots won't be able to penetrate deeply enough.

Possible yield About 6½lb (2.9kg) per 10ft (3m) of row for normal varieties about 10lb (4.5kg) per 10ft (3m) for climbers.

Time from sowing to harvest 12–14 weeks.

Varieties There are three types of French bean; the traditional flat pod, the new fleshy round pods and climbers. For the flat podded, try 'The Prince', the fleshy podded 'Pros Ghana', and of the climbing varieties, 'Hunter'. There are so many new varieties coming out every year, especially of the round/fat podded and climbing sorts, that the only sensible approach is to read about them in the seed catalogues and choose what you want on the basis of that.

Sowing Sow fleshy podded varieties from early May. Flat podded and climbing should be sown from late April. Sow dwarf varieties 2in (5cm) deep, 2–3in (5–7.5cm) apart with 18in (45cm) between rows. Sow climbers 2in (5cm) deep, 6in (15cm) apart with 2ft (60cm) between rows. Sow a few seeds at the end of each plot for filling any gaps. All varieties may also be sown in a greenhouse in pots in mid-April for planting out later.

Transplanting Those raised under glass should be planted out at the above spacings in late May or early June when the risk of frosts is over.

Cultivations Keep weeds down before the complete canopy has formed and smothers them. Never allow the plants to run short of water, especially once the pods are showing. Be ready to protect from frost if the seedlings appear rather too early.

Support climbing varieties with canes as you would runner beans, one cane per seedling soon after they appear or at planting out time.

Pests and diseases Millepedes may attack the seeds, and slugs or cutworms the seedlings at ground level after emergence. Red spider mite can be troublesome in a hot, dry year.

Harvesting Pick regularly and often as soon as the beans start to become ready; if left, they will only spoil. They freeze well, so there's no need to waste a surplus at any one time.

Runner Beans

Runner beans are without a doubt the most economical summer vegetable. Using a modern variety and with good growing, they can be cropping from June/July until the frosts come in the autumn.

Soil requirements The soil should be deeply worked and open to allow the maximum possible root development to sustain cropping over a long period. It should be well supplied with organic matter to increase its water holding capacity and yet maintain good drainage. Many gardeners achieve this by digging out a trench and working garden compost into the bottom before replacing the soil.

Possible yield A good climbing variety can give up to 40lb (18kg) per 10ft (3m) of row; a dwarf variety will yield about half that.

Time from sowing to harvest usually 10–12 weeks.

Varieties Once again, it is hard to keep up with new varieties that crop up every year but 'Red Rum' is consistently good in every respect. For an exhibition variety and for sheer size, Robinsons' 'Liberty' takes a lot of beating. Where there is not enough room for tall varieties, 'Hammonds Dwarf Scarlet' is the time-honoured bush (non-climbing) variety. However, any variety is worth trying so long as you pinch back the shoots as they start to lengthen.

Sowing Early sowings can be made in a heated greenhouse in April, but don't be too early or the plants will be large well before it's safe to plant them out.

Alternatively, sow outdoors *in situ* in late April and cover with cloches or a tunnel. Sow 2in (5cm) deep in double rows, seeds 6in (15cm) apart, rows 2ft (60cm) apart. A third way is to sow outdoors in May without any cover, but be ready to protect the seedlings if a frost threatens. Spacing, again, is 2in (5cm) deep in double rows, seeds 6in (15cm) apart, rows 2ft (60cm) apart.

Because runners grown from this early sowing under cover will finish cropping in the early autumn, a useful trick is to make another sowing in July *in situ* (where they are to grow and crop). With a bit of luck, this will keep you in beans until the first frosts.

Transplanting Harden off and plant outside those raised under heat when all risk of frost is over during May or early June.

Cultivations A 7ft (2m) cane should be pushed in by the side of each seedling on emergence or after planting so that it has something to climb up and so that roots won't be broken later. Tie the cane tops together to a longer cane placed lengthways. An alternative is to use 6ft (1.8m) high plastic bean netting strung between stout posts at each end of the rows. Keep the rows weed-free and always give plenty of water once the beans have started to form.

Pollination and fertilisation is helped if the flowers are sprayed every evening with plain water. It must be remembered, though, that runner beans seldom start to set beans until after the longest day so it doesn't matter how many tricks, etc., you play on them to encourage them to set, they will do it in their own good time, and not before. Once the plants have started cropping, give a top dressing of 'Growmore' to keep their strength up.

In these days of smaller gardens, a very good system is to grow climbing runner beans up tripods as long canes erected in the flower beds. If you take advantage of the different coloured flower varieties, a striking effect can be had, as well as, of course, an excellent vegetable.

Pests and diseases Millipedes may eat the seeds. Blackfly can be a bother late in the summer. Botrytis disease may infect the pods and leaves in a wet summer.

Harvesting Because runner beans freeze well, they should always be picked when they're ready. Pick often and regularly before the seeds have started to swell within the pods. This is seen as slight swellings along the length of the pod. Modern stringless varieties stay in good condition far longer than older ones. Given good conditions and care, they should crop for upwards of three months.

BEETROOT

Another vegetable which is either loved or loathed. Grown for eating cooked, hot or cold or for pickling. Certain varieties (cylindrical in shape) may be stored for the winter.

Soil requirements A light and fertile soil is best for beetroot and all other root crops, but heavy land can be made suitable by adding bulky organic matter, preferably for the preceding crop.

Possible yield In the region of 6½lb (2.9kg) per 10ft (3m) of row for the smaller earlies; 9lb (4kg) or more for maincrop.

Time from sowing to harvest Depending on what you want them for, 12–16 weeks is normal, though those for cooking when large can stay in until you want them.

Varieties 'Boltardy', 'Regala'; both are resistant to bolting. 'Cheltenham Mono' for storing. 'Detroit Little Ball' for pickling and for use when still smell.

Sowing Don't sow unnecessarily early because even the bolt-resistant varieties will run to seed if you abuse them. Sow from April to end of June in drills half an inch deep and either 7in (18cm) apart, for small roots, or 12in (30cm) for maincrop. Sow in late May/early June for winter storage.

Transplanting Never transplant.

Cultivations Thin and single seedlings when large enough to handle. Thin for small roots to 2in (5cm) apart. For maincrop and those for storage, thin to 4in (10cm). This spacing will give a heavy crop of medium sized roots.

Pests and diseases Sparrows destroying the seedlings are probably the worst pest.

Harvesting Pull up earlies when they're little more than golf ball size and maincrop when about tennis ball size. Leave those to be stored until October when they can be either covered with straw or lifted and clamped.

BROCCOLI, SPROUTING

An invaluable spring vegetable and one of the first to be ready after the winter. The plants are very large and require support during the winter. About ten plants should be adequate for an average family.

Soil requirements No special needs, except that heavier soils are preferred. These allow the plants to grow large, but at the same time sturdy.

Possible yield 2–3lb (0.9–1.4kg) per plant, depending on their size.

Time from sowing to harvest About a year.

Varieties Purple sprouting and white sprouting. Early and late variations exist but the difference is insignificant.

Sowing Outdoors in April in nursery rows half an inch deep.

Transplanting Late May to early June. Plant firmly with a dibber, allowing 24–30in (60–75cm) between plants, the greater distance for the earlier plantings. This apparently wide and wasteful spacing is because it leads to stocky and sturdy plants that are less likely to be blown over. Closer planting can draw the plants upwards too much. The plants will still need support. After transplanting, the ground between the young plants can still be used either for a salad crop or for subsequent sowings of brassicas, such as spring cabbage.

Cultivations Water after planting and keep the weeds down. Support with canes when the plants are about 2ft (60cm) tall, well before the winter.

Pests and diseases As for Brussels sprouts. Especially susceptible to pigeons.

Harvesting Start picking the closed flower heads as soon as they are large enough. Keep picking to encourage the formation of more. Don't be frightened of a glut, as sprouting broccoli freezes very well. Picking should stop when the heads become small and the flowers start to grow yellow. This, therefore, is also the time to pull up the plants and compost them. I find it an excellent job for my quiet shredder to chop up the tough, woody, stems. Very satisfying.

BRUSSELS SPROUTS

Sprouts have always been one of the most popular winter green vegetables. They can be grown to give you a supply of sprouts from September to March. Unless you want to strip the plants at a single pick and then freeze the harvest, pick-over varieties should be grown.

Soil requirements The soil should be well-supplied with organic matter and must, if anything, be even firmer than for cabbages or the plants run to leaf and the sprouts will be loose.

Possible yield About 2lb (900g) of sprouts per plant.

Time from sowing to harvest 6–9 months.

Varieties Far better to grow the F1 hybrids than older traditional ones. The varieties given below are suitable for picking over a period but the sprouts can be encouraged to mature more or less together on early varieties by taking out the top of the plants when the bottom sprouts are about a half-inch across, provided that this is before October. This is another vegetable with new varieties coming out every five minutes. At the moment, I grow 'Hastings' if I want an autumn crop, but rely on 'Trafalgar' for early winter and 'Agincourt' and/or 'Revenge' for mid- to late winter. All very blood-thirsty!

Sowing Sow from mid-March to mid-April, according to variety, half an inch deep in nursery rows.

Transplanting Plant very firmly with a dibber from mid-May to early June when the plants are about 6in (5cm) high. Allow 24–30in (60–75cm) between plants, and water the plants well in.

Cultivations Hoe as and when needed to keep the weeds down, and aim at steady growth by watering when required.

Pests and diseases Cabbage root fly, aphids, caterpillars of Large White and Small White butterflies, cabbage moth and club root. In addition, pigeons may be a nuisance in rural areas. Netting the crop is the best means of controlling both pests.

The finer (7mm) net required for butterflies will, of course, keep pigeons at bay during the winter.

Harvesting   Start by picking the lowest sprouts when they are about 1in (2.5cm) across and still hard. This encourages those further up the stem to develop. It is possible to freeze any surplus but they should always be left and then picked later in preference to freezing as they taste better. Also, there is no doubt that sprouts are not at their best until they have had one or two hard frosts on them.

CABBAGES

Cabbage varieties are either round-headed or pointed. They are one of the easiest vegetables to grow because of their tolerance of a wide range of conditions. You can grow a succession of varieties for maturing all the year round.

Soil requirements   No special needs. Cabbages like firm land that is consolidated and well supplied with organic matter.

Possible yield   1–3lb (0.5–1.4kg) per plant.

Time from sowing to harvest   Spring cabbages, 4–6 months. Summer and autumn maturing varieties, 10–17 weeks. Winter, 13–16 weeks.

Varieties   Winter, 'Celtic' or 'Tundra'. Spring (Greens), 'Offenham Wintergreen', (Headed) 'Compacta', 'Flower of Spring', 'Advantage' or 'Pixie'. Summer, 'Hispi' or 'Minicole'. Autumn, 'Minicole'. Winter White, 'Polinius'. Red, 'Ruby Ball'.

Sowing   The soil should be trodden down before sowing. Sow thinly in nursery rows half an inch deep. Sow winter and red varieties outdoors in April/May, spring maturing varieties in July/August. Sow summer varieties under glass in February/March or outdoors in April/June.

Transplanting   Plant firmly using a dibber. Plant out red and winter varieties in June, 18in (45cm) apart. Spring varieties should be transplanted in September/October, 6in (15cm) between plants in the row and 12in (30cm) between rows. In early spring when the plants are touching; take out and use alternate ones, leaving the remainder to mature.

Harden off summer cabbage seedlings raised under glass and plant outside 18in (45cm) apart in April or May. Transplant those raised outdoors in June.

Cultivations   The ground should be well supplied with bulky organic matter which should be incorporated during digging. Lime is beneficial on acid ground. It should be applied soon after digging to allow it to be washed in by the rain. Because of cabbages' liking for firm ground, any digging should have been done well in advance of planting. Hoe regularly to keep the weeds down.

Water in straight after planting, and then as required. Extra watering is only likely to be needed in the summer when a drought can lead to smaller heads and a strong taste.

Pests and diseases   As for Brussels sprouts.

Harvesting   Cabbages are far better if left standing until required for use. However, the Dutch White varieties can be cut and hung upside-down in a shed for use in winter. If you want cabbages in the winter, why not grow 'Celtic', 'Tundra' or 'January King'?

CABBAGE, SAVOY

Easy to grow and very popular in the north of England and in Scotland because of their extreme winter hardiness, savoys are crisp and tasty, with a flavour stronger than that of cabbages. Except in mild districts, grow a few savoys as an insurance against a really bad winter.

Soil requirements As for cabbages.
Possible yield 4–9lb (1.8–4kg) per plant.
Time from sowing to harvest 3–4 months.
Varieties 'January King' and 'Savoy King'.
Sowing and Planting Raise in the same way as winter cabbages by sowing in late April/May and planting out 2ft (60cm) apart in June.
Cultivations and Harvesting As for cabbages.
Pests and diseases As for Brussels sprouts.

CALABRESE

There's always confusion surrounding the difference between calabrese and broccoli. This calabrese (also called American broccoli) is the quick-growing, green headed brassica that matures in the summer and early autumn. An invaluable, quick and easily grown summer vegetable. Depending on the sowing time, it may be had from May/June until September/October.

Soil requirements To ensure the quick growing that is necessary for calabrese to be at its best, the soil should be fertile with plenty of organic matter in it, but not so firm that the roots have to struggle.
Possible yield 1–2lb (0.5–0.9kg).
Time from sowing to harvest About 3 months with cropping, continuing for possibly another 3 months.
Varieties 'Green Comet', 'Corvet', 'Belstar'.
Sowing Should be sown where the plants are to mature. Transplanting can induce small heads and early bolting. Sow from late March to early July for succession.
Cultivations Keep weeds and all competition to a minimum to ensure steady growth and quick maturity. Water as required during the summer.
Pests and diseases As for Brussels sprouts, although pigeons are unlikely to be troublesome.
Harvesting Cut the heads when they are large but before there is a hint of them breaking up. They freeze well so mature heads should never be allowed to remain unpicked. Secondary heads will soon develop so the plants should be left where they are unless the ground is wanted for something more important.

CARROTS

Carrots are indispensable vegetables. Mainly used as mature roots in the winter, they are also a popular summer vegetable when the roots are still young and small.

Soil requirements Light land is always best for carrots as the roots form straight and true. Stony and heavy soil causes the roots to fork, as does land that has recently had manure or compost dug in. On heavy land, grow stump rooted varieties.
Possible yield About 9lb (4kg) of mature roots from a 10ft (3m) run of row, but about half that if you are lifting them earlier.
Time from sowing to harvest From 7 weeks to about 4 months, depending on the variety and when they're lifted.
Varieties For early use, starting at pencil thickness: 'Amsterdam Sweetheart' or 'Nantes Express'. Maincrop: 'Chantenay

Red Cored' (stump rooted) or 'Autumn King' (long rooted). There are also a lot of multi-coloured varieties about now. These are no better than the normal orange ones, and sometimes not as good, but they will add a bit of colour to your life.

Sowing   Earlies may be sown thinly broadcast (not in rows) and raked in from March onward, the earliest being under cloches or cold frames. Sow second-earlies thinly in rows 6in (15cm) apart. Sow maincrop for storing in late April or early May. Sow thinly half an inch deep in rows 8in (20cm) apart.

Transplanting   Never transplant.

Cultivations   Thin second-earlies to 1–2in (2.5–5cm) apart and maincrop to 3–4in (7.5–10cm) as soon as they're large enough to handle. Water in well after thinning to reduce the scent and, thereby, the incidence of carrot fly. Keep watered and growing steadily to prevent splitting and the introduction of disease. Hoe carefully to avoid damage to the carrots. Earth up if the shoulders are showing above the soil, to prevent them going green.

Pests and diseases   Carrot fly is the worst, followed by aphids.

Harvesting   Pull up the earliest as necessary, starting when pencil thickness. Lift maincrop when the tops are dying down in October and store them in clamps or dry in net bags.

CAULIFLOWERS

Not an easy crop to grow well, particularly summer and autumn varieties, because any check to growth, such as drought, usually results in the curds splitting and running up to flowers well before they reach their proper size.

Soil requirements   Their main need is for a deep and fertile soil well supplied with organic matter and deeply dug, preferably well in advance of planting. Rich loams are best but light soils are fine as long as they have good organic matter, moisture and plant food reserves. All these encourage rapid growth and, hence, good quality plants.

Possible yield   2lb (0.9kg) per plant.

Time from sowing to harvest   Varies widely; 3–4 months for summer and autumn varieties, 4–6 months for late autumn varieties and up to a year for those maturing in the spring.

Varieties   Spring maturing, 'Aalsmeer', 'Mayflower'. July–October, 'Aviso'. September–December 'Moby Dick'. As with carrots, there are now some terrific 'coloured' varieties. For example, 'Green Trevi' and 'Alverda' (green), 'Sunset' and 'Cheddar' (orange), 'Graffiti' (reddy purple), 'Violet Queen' and 'Aviron' (pure white). Another favourite of mine is the weirdly-shaped 'Romanesco' cauliflower. 'Veronica' is a good selection but there are several others.

Sowing   Spring maturing varieties, late May. Summer and early autumn, mid-March to late April. Earliest summer crops are from an early February sowing in a heated greenhouse. Autumn, mid-May.

Sow outdoors half an inch deep in a fine tilth. Water the seeds if necessary, and later the seedlings to keep them growing.

Transplanting   Those raised in heat should be hardened off and planted outside in mid-March. Spring maturing varieties, transplant mid-July. Summer & early autumn, mid-May to mid-June. Autumn varieties, late June.

Cultivations   Keep hoeing to kill weeds. Give a pre-planting fertiliser dressing to summer and autumn varieties and never allow them to run short of water. Most varieties that have to stand the winter have self-protecting curds. However, if this is not working very well, snap off an outside leaf and lay it over the curd.

Pests and diseases As for Brussels sprouts.
Harvesting Cut cauliflowers before the curds start to 'blow' (open out), or before that, when you consider them large enough. Cutting in the morning on sunny days stops them going floppy in the heat of a summer's day.

CELERY

Celery is a vegetable with such a characteristic taste that it's not to everyone's liking. Celery stalks may be eaten raw, cooked whole as a vegetable on its own, or chopped up and put in stews. It is, in other words, very versatile. However, it is not an easy vegetable to grow well. Older varieties need to be grown in a trench and earthed up; modern ones don't – they are termed 'self-blanching.'

Soil requirements Bearing in mind that the great celery-growing area in Britain is the Fens, a deep, light soil well supplied with bulky organic matter is ideal. Heavy land is seldom successful unless greatly lightened and improved with bulky organic matter.
Possible yield A well-grown crop should yield 14lb (6.4kg) per 10ft (3m) of row.
Time from sowing to harvest 4–5 months and more, depending on the variety.
Varieties 'Loretta' and 'Galaxy' (self-blanching), 'Victoria' (for trenching).
Sowing Sow in a heated greenhouse, or indoors, in mid-February.
Transplanting Prick out into individual peat pots, still in heat, when large enough to handle, and later into larger pots if necessary. Harden off and plant outside during May or June when the risk of frost is over.
Plant self-blanching varieties in blocks 9in (23cm) apart each way. For trenching (hardier) varieties, dig out a trench 12in (30cm) deep by 15in (37.5cm) wide. Work

plenty of organic matter into the bottom and set the plants 10in (25cm) apart down the middle of the trench. The ridges on the edges of the trench can be used to grow a quick crop of lettuce or radish.
Cultivations A good system with self-blanching celery is to surround the block of plants closely with sacking or black plastic to improve the blanching. Copious watering is needed to prevent the self-blanching varieties becoming tough and stringy – as much as 4 gallons/yd^2 (22l/m^2) a week.
Once trench varieties are about 10in (25cm) tall, loosely tie newspaper round them and fill in the trench to the top of the leaf stalks. Repeat the performance finally in September but be ready to put straw over the leaves once the frosts start.
Pests and diseases Celery fly maggots are the worst. Slugs and snails amongst the leaf stalks.
Harvesting Lift the self-blanching types during the summer and autumn as you need them. When you start using the trenched plants, lift them carefully to avoid damage to the roots of the neighbours. Store a few plants upright in a box under cover before the really cold weather makes it impossible to dig them up.

COURGETTES AND MARROWS

The cultivation of courgettes and marrows is the same in each case; only the size at which they're picked is different – courgettes are simply under-developed marrows. Both are very easy to grow, given the right conditions, but, like other half-hardy vegetables, they are normally raised in heat.

Soil requirements As for cucumbers.
Possible yield Varies enormously but a well-grown plant of a good variety could yield up to 13lb (5.9) kg per plant.

Courgettes.

Time from sowing to harvest 10–12 weeks for courgettes, 12–15 weeks for marrows.

Varieties 'Bambino', 'Defender', Sylvana', 'Soleil' and many more. I must admit that I never bother to grow marrows specifically. I just let the odd courgette grow to full size, if I want one.

Sowing As for cucumbers. In addition, they may also be sown outside where they are to grow. This should be done two seeds per station with 2ft (60cm) between each plant for bush varieties, 4ft (1.2m) for trailing. Sow in the second half of May and be ready to cover the seedlings should there be the prospect of frost at night.

Transplanting Those plants raised in heat can be planted outside when the risk of frost is over. Plant 2ft (60cm) or 4ft (1.2m) apart and always be ready to cover them should the weather turn frosty. Courgettes and marrows also benefit, as do cucumbers, from being planted with the rootball just proud of the ground. This helps to prevent the stem rotting where it comes out of the ground.

Cultivations Keep the plants well watered all the time. To keep the weeds at bay, use a mulch rather than a hoe, thus improving soil moisture retention and avoiding damage to the surface roots.

Pests and diseases Slugs are certainly the worst pest and mildew the worst disease. A problem that sometimes arises is the flower end of the 'fruit' going rotten. This is hard to avoid but is usually only serious in a wet summer. If you leave the dead flower on, the fungus invades it; if you take it off, the fungus invades the wound!

Harvesting Technically, courgettes cease to be courgettes when they are about 6in (15cm) long. However, this could be regarded as extravagant and, in practice, they are picked and used any time *after* they are about 6in (15cm) long.

Marrows must be cut before there is any hint of toughness in the skin; this is usually when they are some 12–14in (30–35cm) long. The best way of judging this is to try to push your thumb nail into the skin on the creases at the stalk end. If you can't do this with ease, you've probably left the marrow too long and it will now be a little too large and coarse.

Although marrows can be stored by hanging them up in a shed after they have matured, this is a waste of time; it is much better to eat them when they're still young, tender and tasty. Always cut marrows and courgettes cleanly from the plant.

CUCUMBERS (OUTDOORS)

Cucumber is another crop that is easier to grow than you would think. The only problem is that outdoor cucumbers tend to have much tougher skins than green-house varieties. Being on the borderline of hardiness, cucumbers always do best when grown against a sunny wall or fence. One of the best ways of growing them outdoors is in a growing-bag; two or three plants per bag. Pots or tubs filled with potting compost is another good way.

Soil requirements   Not a great success in garden soil unless it is more or less 50:50 soil and compost or manure.

Possible yield   If you're lucky, 18–20 cucumbers per plant.

Time from sowing to harvest   3–4 months.

Varieties   'Marketmore' and 'Zelna'.

Sowing   As with tomatoes, even outdoor varieties of cucumber have to be raised in heat in the greenhouse or indoors. Sow two seeds per 2–3in (5–7.5cm) peat pot in mid-April using a good, peat-based seed compost. Pot on into larger pots as necessary.

Transplanting   Because of their suscep-tibility to frost, cucumbers shouldn't be planted outdoors until the risk is over – usually late May or early June. Harden the plants off before planting out.

Allow 24in (60cm) between plants growing in the open garden or three plants per standard growing-bag. Plant so that the top of the rootball is half an inch above the surrounding earth or compost, so that the risk of neck rot is reduced to a minimum.

Cultivations   Cucumbers need even more water than tomatoes. Never allow them to dry out. Feed them according to the instruction on the feed packet, or at least twice a week once they start fruiting.

Train them up canes as a single stem until they get to about 6ft (1.8m) tall, then nip the top out to make sure that they don't over-exert themselves at the expense of size and quality. Another good training system is to fasten bean netting to the wall or fence behind the plants and train two shoots up instead of one. This will mean more feeding and watering of course. If growing the plants along the ground, lay straw down first or cover them with cloches or tunnels. Two shoots per plant are best with this system. These can be encouraged to form by 'stopping' (cut-ting off) the main stem at seven leaves.

Pests and diseases   Cucumbers suffer very few pests or diseases – mildew is likely to be the worst.

Harvesting   Pick the cucumber when the skin has lost most of its wrinkles and before the fruits start to go pale and yellow. They will keep for over a week in the drawer in the bottom of the fridge.

LEEKS

Leeks are hardy winter vegetables with something of an acquired taste; loved by some, hated by others. A long growing season is required, but a good variety will stand the hardest winter weather. They are very easy to grow.

Soil requirements   Tolerant of a very wide range but it should be well drained. The lighter soils make leeks easier to lift.

Possible yield   Depending on the size and variety, about 10lb (4.5kg) per 10ft (3m) of row.

Time from sowing to harvest   7–9 months.

Varieties   'Oarsman', 'Musselburgh' (old, but still good), 'Sultan', 'Elefant'.

Sowing   Sow in February or early March in heat, prick out seedlings and later plant outside. Alternatively, sow thinly *in situ* dur-ing March. Another way is to sow in nursery

Leeks.

rows in March for planting later on. All outdoor sowings are at half an inch depth.

Transplanting Plant heat-raised plants outside when they are about pencil thickness. Thin out and single those sown *in situ*, and plant out (in May) those raised in nursery rows at the same stage. For maximum yield of medium sized leeks, plant out 6in (15cm) apart with 12in (30cm) between rows.

Cultivations When planting out those sown in nursery rows, trim the roots to 1in (2.5cm) long and plant in a 6in (15cm) deep dibber hole. Don't fill in the holes with the dibber but pour in water to settle the plant.

Pests and diseases Onion fly and white rot can be serious in a bad year. If white rot

strikes, don't grow leeks or onions in that place for several years.

Harvesting Lift as required but cover with straw during very cold weather to stop them being frozen into the ground.

LETTUCES

An indispensible crop and the epitome of summer, though they can be grown nearly all year round. No garden should be without a few.

Soil requirements Nothing in particular but avoid land that is too firm or waterlogged. Plenty of organic matter leads to rapid growth and the tastiest lettuces.

Possible yield 12–24 lettuces per 10ft (3m) of row; 24 if the thinnings are eaten.

Time from sowing to harvest 9–12 weeks in the summer.

Varieties I'm not going to be drawn into the trap of recommending any varieties by name. I simply go by what it says in the seed catalogue and what it looks like in the picture. Modern varieties can be large, small or intermediate, crisp or butterhead, or hybrids of the two. However, the greatest advance has been in the so-called 'exotic' varieties. These are all the colours of the rainbow, hearting or pick-over, cos or round. You name it, there's a variety to suit. They can be grown in flowerbeds or containers. A thoroughly versatile crop and one that you should never be without.

Sowing Sow January/February in heat for planting outside later. Alternatively, sow January/February in a frame for planting out later. A third way is to sow March to July outside *in situ*.

Sow in the greenhouse in pots or trays according to the number required. Sow thinly outside half an inch deep in drills 9–12in (22–30cm) apart (12in (30cm) for large, crisp varieties). The most economical way to sow outside is to sow a pinch of seed at the recommended spacing. Single the seedlings to one per station when the strongest one can be seen.

Only sow as many as you think you'll be able to cope with. This may be as few as 6ft (1.8m) of row every fortnight in the summer.

Transplanting Only transplant those raised early in heat or frames, and never after May for fear of bolting. Plant firmly, but with a trowel, not a dibber. Butterheads should be planted 9in (22cm) apart, crisp at 12in (30cm).

Cultivations Those sown *in situ* should be thinned first to half the above planting distances when large enough to handle. Water in well and keep them growing fast.

Once the plants are touching, every other one should be removed to leave the final spacing. The thinnings can be eaten. Keep down the weeds and always give plenty of water.

Pests and diseases Sparrows can play havoc with seedlings. Slugs and aphids can also be troublesome. Botrytis (grey mould) can seriously affect overwintering varieties.

Harvesting Test for maturity (how solid the heads are) by pressing down gently with the back of your hand. Cut when ready.

ONIONS

Bulb Onions

A popular crop, much loved by 'show bench' gardeners. Easy to grow moderately well, but hard to grow to a high standard. Store well for out-of-season use.

Soil requirements Onions prefer light soil that is well drained. Heavy, wet soil encourages large, soft bulbs that won't keep. May be grown from seed or sets (very small onions). Must be firm and fine for best results.

Possible yield About 8lb (3.6kg) from 10ft (3m) of row.

Time from sowing to harvest August sown seeds mature in late June. Spring sown seeds mature in 5–6 months. Spring planted sets mature in 4–5 months.

Varieties 'Sturon' and 'Stuttgarter' are still as good as any if you want to grow them from March planted sets. 'Senshyu' for August-sown seed and 'Red Baron' and 'Bedfordshire Champion' for March-sown seed. For the biggest exhibition onions, 'Kelsae' still rules the roost.

Sowing August or March/April. Sow thinly half an inch deep in rows 12in (60cm) apart.

Planting sets Using the right varieties, plant in March/April 3–4 in (7.5–10cm) apart in rows 10in (25cm) apart for a maximum yield of medium-sized onions.

Cultivations Thin out seedlings when large enough to handle to 2in (5cm) apart. Keep all onions free of weeds. If any bolt, snap off the flower heads.

Pests and diseases White rot fungus and onion fly are their worst enemies.

Harvesting When the leaves have bent over and are turning yellow, the bulbs may be raised with a fork to sever the roots and start the ripening process.

Once the leaves are yellow, the bulbs can be completely lifted and spread out on wire netting above the ground or in a greenhouse to ripen to a finish. Store in net bags or as strings.

Salad Onions

Looking rather like tiny leeks, salad (or green) onions are available throughout most of the growing season from August or spring sowings.

Soil requirements   As for bulb onions.
Possible yield   About 2lb (0.9kg) per 10ft (3m) of row.
Time from sowing to harvest   10–12 weeks from spring sowing.
Varieties   'White Lisbon', 'Summer Isle' and 'Feast'. Good varieties produce hardly any bulb at the base.
Sowing   Sow thinly half an inch deep in rows 4in (10cm) apart. Sow in August/ September or spring and early summer to give a succession of produce.
Cultivations   If necessary, thin the seed-lings to 1in (2.5cm) apart. Keep weed-free and well watered for quick growth.
Pests and diseases   As for bulb onions.
Harvesting   Pull them up when ready and as required.

Pickling Onions

Not widely grown, but a favourite of some people.

Soil requirements   As for bulb onions.
Possible yield   4–5lb (1.8–2.3kg) per 10ft (3m) of row.
Time from sowing to harvest   11–16 weeks.
Varieties   'Paris Silver Skin'.
Sowing   Sow thinly in March/April in rows half an inch deep and 12in (30cm) apart.
Cultivations   Keep weed-free and well watered until foliage starts yellowing.
Pests and diseases   As for bulb onions.
Harvesting   Leave until foliage has dried then lift and dry to a finish under cover. For the show bench, they should be no more than 1in (2.5cm) across.

PARSNIPS

A popular winter root vegetable that makes a change from the ubiquitous winter cab-bages and Brussels sprouts. Easy to grow provided there's a good depth of soil.

Soil requirements   As with carrots, light land is best and stony ground difficult. Nor should it have received manure or com-post immediately beforehand or the roots will fork.
Possible yield   About 9lb (4kg) from 10ft (3m) of row.
Time from sowing to harvest   From 6 months but they're usually left much longer.
Varieties   'Countess', 'Gladiator', 'Tender and True'. The last two show good resis-tance to parsnip canker.
Sowing   Parsnips used to be sown in Feb-ruary but there's little to be gained by this unless you want them for an early autumn show. Sow *in situ* in April or May in rows half an inch deep and 8–12in (20 30cm) apart (the wider for broader varieties).
Transplanting   Never transplant.
Cultivations   When large enough to han-dle, thin the seedlings to 6in (15cm) apart for the larger varieties and 3in (7.5cm) for the smaller (seed catalogues will normally tell you the size of a variety).
Pests and diseases   Carrot fly and aphids may be troublesome. Leaf miner is also seen. Canker is the worst disease.
Harvesting   The flavour is greatly improved if the roots are left in the ground at least until they have been frosted; this turns much of the starch to sugar. Unless the ground is wanted for something else, leave the roots where they are until you want them. Cover them with straw at about Christmas to stop them being frozen into

the ground. If you wish, they can be lifted and stored in clamps in the early winter.

PEAS

A very popular summer vegetable that can be grown in succession to give a supply for most of the summer and early autumn. Surplus can be frozen to give supplies throughout the year. There are now good varieties that can be eaten whole; pod and seeds.

Soil requirements A deep and open soil well supplied with bulky organic matter is needed for peas, or they stop cropping prematurely. Many gardeners achieve this by digging out a trench and working garden compost into the bottom before replacing the soil.

Possible yield Very variable – 4–10lb (1.8–4.5kg) per 10ft (3m) run of row.

Time from sowing to harvest About three months, more than six months if sown in the autumn; though this practice has largely disappeared as it offers no benefits.

Varieties Early: 'Early Onward' or 'Kelvedon Wonder'. Maincrop: 'Hurst Green Shaft'. 'Sugar Snap' can be eaten whole.

Sowing Experienced gardeners sometimes sow in wooden troughs in a heated greenhouse, early to mid-February for planting out later.

Normally, sow *in situ* from late February to late May. Make a drill 6in (15cm) wide and 2in (5cm) deep. For accuracy, sow in two rows within the drill, 3in (7.5cm) between rows and 3in (7.5cm) between seeds. In practice, you may scatter the seeds in the bottom of the drill so that they end up roughly 3in (7.5cm) apart.

Transplanting Only those raised in heat; transplant March.

Cultivations Keep down weeds and water copiously to ensure a heavy crop. As soon as the seedlings are 1–2in (2.5–5cm) high, either put up pea netting along the rows or push twiggy sticks in down the outsides for the plants to climb up. Some varieties are said to require no support; in reality this is not the case.

Pests and diseases Sparrows will peck and seriously damage the seedlings. Pea moth maggots are often found in the pods. Spray with permethrin immediately after flowering.

Harvesting Pick hard and regularly before there's the slightest sign of the pods maturing (drying out and wrinkling). All peas freeze well. Pick 'Sugar Snap' varieties when large but not coarse. If they get too old, they can be podded like normal peas.

POTATOES

Possibly the most widely grown vegetable, they are often quite wastefully grown as they take up a lot of ground that could be used for something more valuable. If space is scarce, grow just a row or two of earlies.

Soil requirements The only thing that potatoes really demand is that the soil is well broken up to allow the tubers to form properly and in a good shape. Plenty of moisture is needed but waterlogging is bad for them.

Possible yield Anything from about 13–22lb(6–10kg) per 10ft (3m) run of row.

Time from sowing to harvest Earlies can be ready in about 3 months, maincrop in about 5 months.

Varieties Early: 'Foremost'. Second early: 'Charlotte', 'Kestrel', 'Marfona'. Early maincrop: 'Picasso'.

Planting   For best and earliest results, the 'seed' tubers should be laid out (egg trays are good for this) in the warmth indoors to form sprouts. Plant the tubers when the shoots are about 1in (2.5cm) long and when the risk of frosts is nearly over. Take out 'V' trenches about 6in (15cm) deep and 24–30in (60–75cm) apart for the tubers to be planted in. Allow 12–15in (30–37.5cm) between tubers. Earlies can go at the two closer spacings, maincrop at the wider.

Cultivations   Because of their susceptibility to frost, you should be ready to protect the top growth once it is through. Old bed sheets, polythene or straw are perfectly adequate for this. Once the tops are about 9in (23cm) tall, start earthing them up by drawing the soil up over them in the row. This protects them from any late frost and encourages tubers to form on the section of recently buried stem.

Earth up again when the tops are another 6–9in (15–23cm) taller. This will encourage more tubers and also keep the weeds down. This process is what has given rise to the rather odd statement that potatoes are a 'cleaning' crop; it's simply the cultivations that occur when earthing up.

When the young tubers are about 1in (2.5cm) across, keep the crop really well watered (as mentioned in Chapter 6) to fill up the tubers.

Pests and diseases   Wireworm are the worst pests, potato blight is the worst disease.

Harvesting   There are lots of old wives' tales about the correct stage of growth at which to lift potatoes, such as when they're in flower. The only reliable way to tell when they're ready is to scrape some earth away and have a look. Earlies should be lifted as you need them once they're large enough to make it worthwhile. Leave maincrop until you need them but lift any remaining in mid-October for fear of frost and the increased likelihood of blight. Although lifted maincrop potatoes can be clamped, this can be an awful sweat; storing them in paper sacks from the greengrocer is much easier and handier.

RADISHES

A valuable summer salad crop. Very useful for inter-cropping. There's also a hardy selection for winter use. Very easy to grow but needs good soil and moisture.

Soil requirements   Plenty of organic matter, open and fertile.

Possible yield   About 4.5lb (2kg) per 10ft (3m) of row. Much more than that is produced by the larger winter varieties.

Time from sowing to harvest   4–6 weeks for the normal varieties.

Varieties   For summer use: 'Prinz Rotin', firm (not hollow) but not woody, and slow to bolt. 'Scarlet Globe.' For winter use: 'Black Spanish Round'.

Radishes.

Sowing   Sow fortnightly from March to mid-June for summer crops, late July and throughout August for the winter ones. Sow thinly, half an inch deep and not too much at any one time; 6ft (1.8m) of row should be ample. Winter radishes should be thinned progressively to about 6in (15cm) apart, using the thinnings.

Transplanting   Never transplant.

Cultivations   Keep weed-free and well fed and watered to encourage quick growth.

Pests and diseases   Flea beetle will attack seedling leaves. Cabbage root fly are also a danger.

Harvesting   Pull summer varieties when ready and well before they get old and coarse. Winter radishes can be left until wanted or lifted in October/November and stored in sand like carrots.

SHALLOTS

Not as popular as they should be, even though they are a very good substitute for onions. They are terribly easy to grow.

Soil requirements   Good soil is needed for the best crops but they are tolerant of most types.

Possible yield   About 10lb (4.5kg) from every 10ft (3m) of row.

Time from sowing to harvest   4–6 months.

Varieties   'Giant Long Keeping Yellow' for heaviest yield. 'Hative de Niort' for exhibition-standard shallots. 'Matador' can be grown from seed.

Planting   Plant so that only the tops are visible in March. Allow 6in (15cm) between bulbs, 10–12in (25–30cm) between rows.

Cultivations   Hoe to keep weeds down but take care not to catch the bulbs with the blade. Draw the soil away from the base of the climps when they're nearly mature to help ripening.

Pests and diseases   As for onions.

Harvesting   Once the leaves have died down in the summer, lift the bulbs, dry them off as you would onions and store them in a bag in an airy place. Keep aside enough of the smallest for planting the following spring.

SPINACH

True spinach, as opposed to New Zealand Spinach and Spinach Beet is a quick-growing summer vegetable rich in vitamins and iron. The cartoon character Popeye is probably its greatest devotee! Not the easiest crop to grow because of its liability to bolt at the slightest provocation.

Soil requirements   A deep, rich soil well supplied with organic matter and nitrogen is needed to ensure that the crop grows quickly. On poor soil, the plants are weak and will bolt prematurely. It is a useful quick-growing vegetable for intercropping.

Possible yield   About 8oz (225g) per plant.

Time from sowing to harvest   6–10 weeks.

Varieties   'Bloomsdale' and 'Matador'.

Sowing   Sow thinly 1 in (2.5cm) deep every 2–3 weeks from March to July to give a continuous supply. If the weather is slow to warm up, delay the early sowings as they will usually bolt.

Transplanting   Never transplant.

Cultivations   When the seedlings are large enough to handle, thin them to 3in (7.5cm) apart and later, when they touch, to 6in (15cm). Of the plants thinned later, the removed plants can be used. Thinning is an important deterrent to bolting. Be generous with water during dry spells to encourage quick and even growth.

Pests and diseases   Aphids may be troublesome but little else is.

Harvesting   Once the outer leaves are large enough, pick them regularly and before they get tough. This will lead to the constant production of new leaves.

SPINACH, NEW ZEALAND

Unrelated to true spinach, New Zealand (or prickly) spinach is a very hardy winter vegetable which has the added benefit of being largely drought resistant. It forms a creeping plant with fleshy, arrow-shaped leaves. It doesn't bolt.

Soil requirements   As for true spinach.

Possible yield   Up to 2lb (0.9kg) per plant.

Time from sowing to harvest   Minimum of seven weeks.

Varieties   'New Zealand'.

Sowing   Sow from mid-May until mid-September half an inch deep, but instead of sowing in rows, sow three or four seeds in a clump with 2ft (60cm) between clumps.

Transplanting   Don't transplant.

Cultivations   When the seedlings are large enough to handle, thin them out to leave just the strongest plant in each station.

Nip out the tips of the shoots when the plants are about 1ft (30cm) across to encourage branching and, hence, more leaves. In wet autumns, it helps to either cloche the plants or straw the ground beneath them to avoid mud splash.

Pests and diseases   Nothing specific, but keep your eyes open for greenfly and caterpillars.

Harvesting   Both the leaves and soft ends of the stems are edible, so constant picking encourages more to grow.

SPINACH BEET

One of the many edible members of the beet family. Winter hardy are eaten in late winter and during the spring until they run up to flower (bolt). Spinach 'Perpetual' beet doesn't bolt until after the winter and has a milder flavour than true spinach.

Soil requirements   Although tolerant of sandy and other poor soils, spinach beet is at its best on deep, moist land well supplied with organic matter.

Possible yield   At least 1lb (0.5kg) per plant, more if it is picked hard.

Time from sowing to harvest   In theory, about seven weeks, but it is normal to leave the plants for late winter/early spring use.

Varieties   'Perpetual'. As with lettuces, leaf beet has not escaped the colour revolution. The supreme example is 'Bright Lights' – an explosion of colour from white, through yellow and orange, to pale and dark red. This will brighten up the drabbest vegetable patch and I find that, even in Yorkshire, it is normally winter-hardy.

Sowing   Can be sown in the spring for a summer crop, but these plants usually end up much too big. Best sown during July for winter and spring use. Sow *in situ* in rows 1 in (2.5cm) deep with, if required, 18in (45cm) between rows.

Transplanting   Don't transplant.

Cultivations   Thin the seedlings when they are large enough to handle. Either thin to 4in (10cm) apart and later to 8in (20cm), cooking the second thinnings; alternatively, thin just once to 8in (20cm).

Pests and diseases   None in particular.

Harvesting   You can start picking in the summer when the outside leaves are large enough but, if wanted for later use, don't overdo it or you'll simply send the plants into the winter small and weak.

SWEDES

Not as popular vegetables as they might be and normally found in the north of England rather than the south. Swede is a very pleasant change in the winter from other more mundane things. Oddly, swedes seem to grow better by the acre than in gardens.

Soil requirements   No particular likes and, unlike carrots and parsnips, perfectly at home on heavy and stony ground.
Possible yield   About 11lb (5kg) from 10ft (3m) of row.
Time from sowing to harvest   Three months, but the roots will stay in the ground safely for a further seven, until March.
Varieties   'Marian'.
Sowing   Sow from mid-May to mid-June (the earlier in the colder north of Britain). Sow ¾–1 in (2–2.5cm) deep in rows 15–18in (37.5–45cm) apart.
Transplanting   Don't transplant.
Cultivations   Thin to 9in (23cm) apart as soon as the seedlings are large enough to handle. Swede tops make a pleasant spring vegetable. To get a supply of these, leave part of a row unthinned and use it only for tops.
Pests and diseases   Cabbage root fly; also club root and mildew, but 'Marian' less susceptible than other varieties.
Harvesting   Start lifting swedes as soon as they're large enough to eat in the late summer. For preference, leave them in the ground until you want them; they're

perfectly hardy. If you need the land, they can be lifted in early winter and clamped.

SWEET CORN

Not everyone's choice for a garden vegetable, because they take up rather a lot of room and are only moderately successful in a poor British summer. Varieties are constantly improving, however. Sweet corn likes a damp July and a warm August.

Soil requirements   A wide range is tolerated but it must be well drained and must warm up quickly in spring as sweet corn doesn't grow well at soil temperatures below 50°F (10°C)
Possible yield   1–2 cobs per plant.
Time from sowing to harvest   About four months.
Varieties   This is another vegetable that has undergone much improvement in the

Sweetcorn.

last fifteen to twenty years; mainly with the introduction of 'supersweet' varieties. 'Early Extra Sweet' (supersweet), 'Royalty' (normal sugar) and 'Sweet Nugget' (supersweet) are all well suited to cooler conditions.

Sowing   May be sown singly in peat pots in heat during April or outdoors *in situ* in the first half of May.

Sow outdoors, 10in (25cm) between seeds, in rows 30in (75cm) apart. It's as well to sow several more in peat pots to allow for any gaps. Aim to get as near square a plot as possible because sweet corn is wind pollinated and this assists it. Added to that, it gives the plants good wind protection as they support each other.

Transplanting   Plant out heat-raised plants when the risk of frost is over at the spacings quoted above.

Cultivations   Cloches and tunnels are a terrific help in the early stages to get the seeds and seedlings started and growing away. Keep weed-free with a good thick mulch of garden compost; hoeing should be avoided as it can easily damage the shallow root system.

Pests and diseases   Nothing in particular.

Harvesting   The cobs are ripe when the 'silks' that hang from the top are drying and have gone brown, but before the covering of the cob has started to turn yellow. A further test is to expose the top of the cob and test an individual seed. If it is still milky, leave it a few more days. It is safest to use secateurs to cut the cob from the plant. Any surplus can be frozen on the cob.

SWEET PEPPERS (CAPSICUMS)

Although it is more successful to grow peppers in a greenhouse, modern varieties will give perfectly acceptable results in the open if grown in the warmest part

Peppers.

of a garden against a south-facing wall or fence. The sweet pepper is another of those vegetables that have grown in popularity in the last ten to fifteen years. Their cultivation is easy and very similar to that of tomatoes.

Soil requirements   Hardly worth bothering to grow them in ordinary soil; much better to use growing bags or peat-based potting compost in large (9in/22cm) pots.

Possible yield   You could expect anything over 2lb (0.9kg) per plant in a good summer.

Time from sowing to harvest   About five months.

Varieties   'Atris', 'Mavras' and 'New Ace.' Hot varieties include 'Chilli Long Slim' and several others.

Sowing   Because the plants are slower growing and smaller than tomatoes, they can be sown earlier, the second half of March being suitable if sufficient heat is available to germinate the seeds and maintain growth.

As with tomatoes, sow two seeds per 3in (7.5cm) of peat pot and remove the weaker seedling when it is seen. Keep watering to a minimum until growth is going well.

Transplanting Always keep peppers under glass as long as you can and, in any event, until the end of May. This allows the plants to grow for longer in the warmth before being planted outside. Allow three plants per growing bag. The best system is to plant in the bag as soon as the plants outgrow their pots and keep the bag under cover until the space is wanted for something else.

Cultivations Protect the plants with a polythene covering when newly moved outside. Keep well watered at all times and fed as for tomatoes.

Pests and Diseases Nothing really to worry about.

Harvesting Most varieties of pepper attain full size when still green. They can be cut and used at this stage or may be left until they are partially or completely red. Oddly enough, they freeze very well whole, but can, of course only be used for cooking after thawing.

TOMATOES (OUTDOORS)

A far easier crop to grow than most beginners would believe, the outdoor tomato is always economical and well worth growing. The main benefit of growing your own is that a much better choice of varieties, and hence flavour, is open to you. They are always best when grown against a wall. If only a small amount of space is available, I believe it's much better to use growing-bags. If you're growing single-stemmed varieties, reckon on four per bag; three for bush varieties.

Soil requirements If grown in the open garden, the soil must be deep, open, fertile and well supplied with organic matter. It is usually far better and wiser to use growing bags.

Possible yield If all goes well, around 4.5lb (2kg) per plant.

Time from sowing to harvest 4–5 months.

Varieties 'Gardener's Delight' is still one of the best varieties. 'Golden Sunrise' has a terrific flavour. For one of those lumpy and large Continental tomatoes, go for 'Marmande'.

Sowing Sow in heat (63°F / 17°C) in a greenhouse or indoors in mid-April. Best to sow two seeds in small individual peat pots and retain the stronger seedling when large enough to distinguish.

Transplanting Pot on into 4in (10cm) pots when the smaller ones are full of root. Harden off and plant in final position when first flowers are open, or after the risk of frost is over.

If planting in the open garden, allow 18in (45cm) between plants and 24in (60cm) between rows. A standard sized growing bag will hold three bush plants and four trained plants outdoors.

Cultivations Bush varieties don't have to be trained but will need the support of a stake to tie the main shoots to as they develop.

Varieties requiring training should be tied to a stout cane or stake alongside them and should be grown as a single stem, all side shoots being removed as soon as they're seen. They should be allowed to produce four fruit trusses, and then the tops should be nipped out leaving two leaves above the fourth truss. Control any weeds and keep the plants well supplied with water at all times. Feed according to the instructions on the feed bottle.

As bush varieties start to fruit, lay straw on the ground beneath them to stop the fruits getting mud splashed. As the autumn approaches, cut the plants away from their support, lay them on straw and put cloches or a tunnel over them to help them ripen.

Pests and diseases   Potato blight is one of the few problems.

Harvesting   Tomatoes may be picked once the whole fruit is coloured but when they are still too hard to eat. Ripen them indoors.

TURNIPS

Not to everyone's taste, but a popular root vegetable available from about May to October, according to sowing time. Found with either white or yellow flesh.

Soil requirements   No particular fancies but light, moist, well-drained soils are best.

Possible yield   About 9lb (4kg) per 10ft (3m) of row.

Time from sowing to harvest   2–3 months.

Varieties   'Golden Ball', 'Purple Top Milan'. 'Market Express', one of the fastest growing turnips, can be ready about fifty days from sowing.

Sowing   From March to mid-July to produce roots from May to October. Sow three-quarters of an inch deep in rows 1ft (30cm) apart.

Transplanting   Don't transplant.

Cultivations   Thin the seedlings to 4in (10cm) apart as soon as they can be handled. Keep weed-free and well watered to promote quick and tender growth. This is particularly important with the earlies which should be eaten before they get too large.

Pests and diseases   Flea beetle, cabbage root fly, club root and mildew.

Harvesting   If you're growing a crop for earlies only, pull them when they're from golf ball to tennis ball size. Leave maincrop until October/November, then lift and clamp them or store in dry sand or peat.

Useful Addresses

Spray Chemicals and Weedkillers

The Scotts Co. Ltd.
Salisbury House
Weyside Park
Godalming
Surrey
GU7 1XE

Bayer Garden

230 Cambridge Science Park
Milton Road
Cambridge
CB4 0WB

Sprayers

Hozelock Sprayers Ltd.
Midpoint Park
Birmingham
B76 1AB

Pruning Equipment

Burton McCall Ltd.
163 Parker Drive
Leicester
LE4 0JP

Darlac

P.O. Box 996
Slough
Berks
SL3 9JF

Index

Other Gardening Books from Crowood

Cunningham, Sally, *Ecological Gardening*
Gray, Linda, *Herb Gardening*
Gregson, Sally, *Ornamental Vegetable Gardening*
Gregson, Sally, *Practical Propagation*
Hodge, Geoff, *Pruning*
Jones, Peter, *Gardening on Clay*
Littlewood, Michael, *The Organic Gardener's Handbook*
Marder, John, *Water-Efficient Gardening*
Nottridge, Rhoda, *Wildlife Gardening*
Saunders, Bridgette, *Allotment Gardening*